THE LITTLE BOOK of GRATITUDE

for Latter-day Saints

OTHER BOOKS AND AUDIOBOOKS
BY ED J. PINEGAR

Press Forward Saints

Living by the Word

Your Patriarchal Blessing

Happily Ever After

Power Tools for Missionaries, Four Volumes

After Your Mission

Lengthen Your Shuffle

Series of Latter-Day Commentaries, Teachings and Commentaries, Unlocking, and Who's Who—Old Testament, New Testament, Book Mormon, and Doctrine and Covenants

The Temple: Gaining Knowledge and Power in the House of the Lo

The Christmas Code

The Christmas List

Preparing for the Melchizedek Priesthood and My Mission

The Little Book of Gratitude

31 Days to a Better You

Fatherhood: A Calling of Love

It's Great to Be a Missionary

Living after the Manner of Happiness

Because of Him

God the Father: Our Loving and Compassionate Heavenly Father

THE LITTLE BOOK of GRATITUDE

for Latter-day Saints

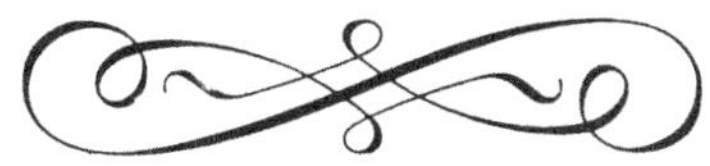

Ed J. Pinegar

Covenant Communications, Inc.

Cover image: *Autumn Foliage* © Borut Trdina, courtesy istockphoto.com

Published by Covenant Communications, Inc.
American Fork, Utah

Printed in the United States of America
First Printing: September 2016

11 10 9 8 7 6 5 4

ISBN 978-1-68047-961-4

Ed Pinegar is not only a fine writer, but he is also a fine man. He lives what he teaches others. I highly recommend this little gem of a book to anyone who wants to feel better about life, see another world, and generally be more happy and satisfied. Gratitude reduces stress, competition, and envy. It heals and helps everyone feel better. Ed's knowledge and beliefs beautifully illustrated in this book are born of inspiration!

—Elaine S. Dalton, former Young Women General President

Finally a book on that most neglected of all virtues. We live in a self-serving society that has forgotten the power and purpose of gratitude. For many, entitlement has replaced the thankful heart, and consequently the love of men has waxed cold. Somehow gratitude must be reenthroned in the hearts of humanity, for it has the power to heal marriages, soften the heart of the wayward child, invoke the influence of the Spirit, and allow us to lay hold upon the merciful gift of Christ's Atonement. Thank you, Brother Ed, for reminding us of the place this holy virtue must have in the hearts of all those who seek to have the image of God engraven in their countenances.

—Alonzo L. Gaskill, Ph.D., associate professor of Church history and doctrine, BYU

Table of Contents

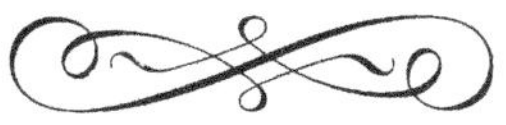

Foreword

I FIRST MET ED PINEGAR almost forty-eight years ago. He radiated light—the kind of light that attracts others. And his wife! She too was happy and positive and busy supporting her bishop husband and little family.

I was a new student at BYU, and Ed Pinegar was my bishop. From the start, he greeted me by name with warmth and genuine love.

After a month at BYU, my father passed away. I was devastated and discouraged. Several days after my father's funeral, I received a note attached to a beautiful flower arrangement, which said: "If there is anything I can do to help you, I am here. Your bishop, Ed Pinegar." All these years later, I remember those words written on a small card and the reassurance they gave and still give me today.

I feel such a deep sense of gratitude for Ed. He will always be "my bishop," my friend, my example, and my mentor. He has served as a bishop, a mission president, and a temple president, and has filled numerous other positions and callings. But above all, he is a disciple who loves the Lord and lights the way for others. Perhaps there is no greater expression of true gratitude for our Savior, Jesus Christ, than to follow Him and pattern our lives after His. This is what Ed does.

I am grateful for this little book. In it I believe the reader will be tutored on the blessings that come from cultivating a grateful heart. The scripture admonishes us to "give thanks in all things" (Mosiah 26: 38–39), and when we learn to do this, we see adversity and trials in relationship to the great plan of happiness. Indeed there is always something to be thankful for. Ed taught me that, and his words in this book will do the same for you.

> "What greater gift dost thou bestow,
> What greater goodness can we know
> Than Christ-like friends, whose gentle ways
> Strengthen our faith, enrich our days."

—Elaine S. Dalton
Former Young Women General President

Gratitude Can Turn . . .

Adversity into Opportunity
Discouragement into Hope
Envy into Charity
Sorrow into Joy
Jealousy into Love
An Enemy into a Friend
Weakness into Strength
Restlessness into Peace
Doubt into Faith
Helplessness into Prayer
Trials into Blessings
Hatred into Love
Pride into Humility
Greed into Generosity
Selfishness into Caring

Acknowledgments

With *gratitude* I express my appreciation for all my wonderful friends and editors who have made this work possible. I am grateful to Richard J. Allen, with whom I have written many books. I am especially grateful for my superb and insightful editor Kristin McQuivey, who has contributed so much to the rebirth of this book. Special thanks to my dear friends Samantha Millburn and Kathy Gordon, who have so faithfully stood by me to make my works become the very best. To my sweetheart, Pat, who is so supportive of my time spent hunched over the computer, typing with my three fingers—I am forever grateful for you. And always I am grateful to acknowledge the hand of God in all things, for which I praise and thank my Heavenly Father and my Savior each day.

Introduction

CICERO CALLED GRATITUDE THE PARENT of all the other virtues. Indeed, that is true, but gratitude is also, ironically, the most forgotten virtue. It's easy, then, to see why so many of us do not practice basic gratitude, for to possess a deep sense of gratitude requires real effort.

Nevertheless, if we are willing to work at gratitude, the power it unlocks in our lives can be tremendous. Sincere appreciation helps us access a whole range of temporal and spiritual blessings. Gratitude invigorates the soul. It overcomes fear, envy, and resentfulness. It frees the heart to love others and be concerned with more than self. It fills the heart with joy for the success of others. The deeper our appreciation, the clearer we see with the eyes of the Savior and the more our life connects with our Heavenly Father.

Gratitude is an empowering virtue. The Lord has commanded us to live in thanksgiving daily. As Amulek taught, "Humble yourselves even to the dust, and worship God, in whatsoever place ye may be in, in spirit and in truth; and that ye live in thanksgiving daily, for the many mercies and blessings which he doth bestow upon you" (Alma 34:38). Like all things the Lord asks us to do, this commandment entails myriad promised blessings when we keep it.

Elder James E. Talmage once observed that "God requires thanksgiving, praise and worship, not for His gratification as the recipient of adulation, but for the good of His children" (*Sunday Night Talks*, 2nd ed. [Salt Lake City: The Church of Jesus Christ of Latter-day Saints, 1931], 486). The good we receive by developing a thankful heart is immeasurable. It cultivates feelings of reverence for God and, thereby, opens our souls to the influence of the Holy Spirit. It allows us to find joy in the here and now. A thankful heart allows us to face trials firm in the knowledge of our Heavenly Father's love for us. I like the words of Carolyn Wright concerning the power of gratitude: "The grateful heart," she says, "sits at a continual feast" ("The Thankful Heart," *Ensign*, March 1994).

Remember that Moroni's promise is not just one of learning of the truthfulness of the Book of Mormon but is also one of gratitude itself; remember that he exhorted us to ponder on the mercy and goodness of the Lord—that is, to be grateful: "Behold, I would exhort you that when ye shall read these things, if it be wisdom in God that ye should read them, that ye would remember how merciful the Lord hath been unto the children of men, from the creation of Adam even down until the time that ye shall receive these things, and ponder it in your hearts" (Moroni 10:3). Moroni wanted us to understand and appreciate the goodness and mercy of the Lord so our hearts would be full of gratitude. Through this thankfulness, we would be drawn to Him and seek to accept His love by receiving His infinite Atonement into our lives. A righteous life begins first and foremost with a grateful heart. There are portions of gratitude exerting power in every aspect of our lives. Within all virtues, we will find elements of thanksgiving. As you read this little book, I hope you will begin to notice more frequently the innumerable reasons we have to be grateful and how gratitude enlivens our lives and brings joy to our souls.

The Gratitude Journal

Throughout this book, I will include questions and journaling ideas. I call these prompts "Journaling Moments of Joy." It is my hope that you will keep a notebook and pen nearby as you read. Keep track of all the things you are thankful for; write them down. Keeping a gratitude journal will bless your life and will show you the empowering nature of gratitude. These exercises, found throughout this book, are truly invaluable and key to living in gratitude. Whenever you see the heart icon, grab your notebook and write a few lines.

Why is this so important? Because you don't just all of a sudden have a grateful heart. You have to cultivate it. That is why Moroni tells us in Moroni 10:3 to ponder on the mercies of the Lord from the time of Adam until today. You cannot have the blessing of gratitude if you don't work at understanding, appreciating, and recording your grateful feelings. You'll feel grateful here and there, hit and miss. But when it happens, when you truly *become* grateful, it becomes part of your heart and soul. It's just what you are and what you do. And when that happens, you will feel so great! You are immediately blessed. Like King Benjamin tells us, if you do these things, God will immediately bless you.

So join with me. Grab a notebook and a pen, find a comfy reading spot, and let the Lord bless your life as you discover the heavenly virtue of gratitude.

PART I:

Planting the Seeds of Gratitude

Chapter 1
THE VISION OF GRATITUDE

The Nature of Gratitude

GRATITUDE IS THE QUALITY OF being thankful. It is the fundamental virtue to a happy and fulfilling life. It is multifaceted and empowering. It is a key to righteousness, the catalyst of change, and an empowering virtue to motivate us to do good.

As we live in thanksgiving daily, our journals can become a source of strength if we take time to record and reread those precious words that bind us to our Heavenly Father, our Savior, and those we love.

Journaling Moment of Joy

Begin your gratitude journal by recording your feelings about gratitude and listing those for whom you are grateful.

> *Life is to be loved and lived with gratitude.*

Life is to be loved and lived with gratitude. A grateful heart will help us live to learn, learn to love, and then love to live. Life is to be lived with a sense of joy and happiness; indeed, "Men are, that they might have joy" (2 Nephi 2:25). But in order to access that joy, we need to learn what matters most and then seek the happy road that can bless and help others as well as ourselves. As Elder Marvin J. Ashton has taught:

> Generally speaking, those inclined to count their blessings have more to count because they help make more possible as they learn gratitude. A constant waiting for a brighter future may cause us to lose the beautiful today. Some spend so much time getting ready to live for an unknown future that too late they discover there is no time to live. Very often in our anxiousness for the joys of the future we run away from the very things we are wanting and needing

today. An appropriate examination of the passing moment will prove it leads to eternity. We need to constantly remind ourselves eternity is in process now. ("The Time is Now," *Ensign*, May 1975)

Find joy in the process. How do we make this process here on earth successful? With a grateful heart. There are many blessings that come from eternal truths residing in our hearts. Here are just a few of them (emphasis added):

- We become sanctified because *we have yielded our hearts to God* (see Helaman 3:35)
- We love *with all of our hearts* (see Matthew 22:37; D&C 4:2)
- We have an *understanding heart* that is *the wellspring of life* (see Proverbs 16:22)
- *When our heart is pure*, we can see God (see 3 Nephi 12:8)
- The word of God was engraved upon the plates in hopes that we *would receive them with thankful hearts* (see Jacob 4:3)
- "And it came to pass that there was no contention in the land, *because of the love of God which did dwell in the hearts of the people*. And

> there were no envyings, nor strifes, nor tumults, nor whoredoms, nor lyings, nor murders, nor any manner of lasciviousness; and surely there could not be a happier people among all the people who had been created by the hand of God" (4 Nephi 1:15–16)

A grateful heart is a beginning, a result, and an innate quality of all other virtues if we have eyes to see and a heart to feel.

We need to have our eyes, our ears, our mind, and our very soul focused on our blessings, expressing gratitude and thanksgiving to our Heavenly Father daily, and expressing gratitude to others. A person who lives with thanksgiving looks at life with a pure heart and soul. The lens of gratitude brings inherent blessings to our lives. It becomes rooted in our very beings and becomes part of us. Our heart is changed, and we possess a most precious gift from God—a loving and grateful heart.

Gratitude can sustain us, especially when we feel we have the least to be grateful for. As President Dieter F. Uchtdorf has taught us:

Gratitude transcends whatever is happening around us. It surpasses disappointment, discouragement, and despair. It blooms just as beautifully in the icy landscape of winter as it does in the pleasant warmth of summer. When we are grateful to God *in* our circumstances, we can experience gentle peace in the midst of tribulation. In grief, we can still lift up our hearts in praise. In pain, we can glory in Christ's Atonement. In the cold of bitter sorrow, we can experience the closeness and warmth of heaven's embrace. We sometimes think that being grateful is what we do *after* our problems are solved, but how terribly shortsighted that is. How much of life do we miss by waiting to see the rainbow before thanking God that there is rain? Being grateful in times of distress does *not* mean that we are pleased with our circumstances. It *does* mean that through the eyes of faith we look beyond our present-day challenges. This is not a gratitude of the lips but of

> the soul. It is a gratitude that heals the heart and expands the mind. ("Grateful in Any Circumstance," *Ensign*, May 2014)

Journaling Moment of Joy

Take a moment to ponder President Uchtdorf's inspiring words. Record your feelings. Miraculous things happen when we are grateful in the midst of trials and tribulation.

It is through opposition, adversity, and severe trials—where we are tested and stretched to the breaking point—that gratitude fills our soul and empowers us to overcome and handle the adversities of life.

While serving in the Manti Utah Temple, I met a wonderful couple, the Mendenhalls, who had served a mission in Nauvoo, Illinois. They had stayed in the home their great-grandfather built, and it was a very special time for them. During their mission, they faced many unanticipated and difficult setbacks that brought gratitude into their lives. Terry Mendenhall gave permission for me to share a letter she wrote containing her story:

My mission to Nauvoo was one of the most inspiring and spiritual experiences I have ever had. Even though I broke my ankle a week after arriving in Nauvoo and had two bouts of pneumonia, I always felt my spirit strengthening. If I wasn't contagious and I could get out of the house, I went to all of my assignments and sites. The Lord really sustained me.

However, on December 6, two days before leaving my mission for home, I was fighting for my life.

That day was the annual Old Nauvoo Christmas walk, where all of Nauvoo comes together to enjoy stories, caroling, and other activities. I was assigned to go caroling for an hour. In various spots along the side of the road were old-time fire barrels. It was a cold night, with temperatures well below freezing. While waiting for some of our caroling group to arrive, I turned my back to the fire to get warm. I had my pioneer dress on, and knowing that fire was the second leading cause of death for pioneer women, after childbirth, I stayed a few feet away from the barrel. Even with my precaution, a gust of wind must have caused the fire to jump onto my dress, and I heard someone yell, "You're on fire! Drop and roll!" The fire ignited my cotton dress so fast the flames went above my head in seconds, and no one could get to me. I didn't know how to get down for fear the fire would burn the front of me. Enveloped by flames and thinking I was going to die, someone tackled me from the front and pushed me straight back. I hit my head hard. Those around me tried to put the fire out with their gloved hands, and just when they thought they were fighting a losing battle, they extinguished the flames.

Someone called 911, and I was life-flighted to the Iowa City Burn Unit. I had third-degree burns from my waist down. Because I had my coat on, my back wasn't burned, and the doctors were able to take grafts from my back and staple them on my burns. A week later they extracted over 250 staples from those grafts and scrubbed my burns. I thought the worst pain in my life was giving birth to six children naturally; however, the pain of those births didn't even come close to the pain I experienced with these burns. The doctors told me it would take at least a year to heal and that I would be scarred for life. I didn't care. I was so grateful to be alive.

I knew I was blessed, and I never asked, "Why me?" throughout this ordeal. There were so many miracles.

Why my hair didn't catch fire is a mystery and a miracle. The doctors were amazed I didn't contract an infection, considering how extensive my burns were. They were also surprised at how quickly I was healing.

For the first two months after the fire, I thought one of the elders had tackled me to the ground. I was finally told that no one tackled me because the flames were so high. However, I know I felt a tackle. I now believe my mother, who had died five months earlier, tackled me and saved my life.

I am so, so grateful to my Heavenly Father for all the miracles He has wrought in my behalf. I'm so grateful for the power of prayer and fasting. I was told my name was put in almost every temple in the world. Wards that didn't even know me were fasting and praying for me, and even the wonderful congregations of the Catholics and Protestants in Nauvoo prayed for me. I am so very grateful for the power of the priesthood. Believe it or not, I am grateful for the experience of being burned because of all the love I felt, the miracles I received, and especially the lessons I learned about myself and the kingdom of my Father in Heaven.

The true test of our gratitude comes not when things are good (though too many of us fail at that easy test) but when things are hardest. If we are grateful even in our most difficult circumstances,

> *With hope and gratitude, we will see that we can overcome our trials and tribulations.*

not only can our souls be comforted, but we will also be empowered by the grace of God to overcome and conquer our challenges.

Turning adversity into opportunity becomes a test all of us must face. With hope and gratitude, we will see that we can overcome our trials and tribulations.

* * *

One of my friends and former students Lee Ann has lived through many trials. This is her story:

> I was born and raised in Ontario, Canada. I had an idyllic childhood, full

of large, extended-family gatherings and summers spent on the lake. When I was seventeen years old, I met the missionaries and joined the Church. I attended and graduated from BYU, got married, and moved back to Canada.

What happened during the next years of my life couldn't have been further from the safe, protected childhood I had experienced. One day when I was running errands, my husband took our two young children and left the country. For six months, I lived in indescribable anguish and did not know if I would ever see my children again. Once I was finally, gratefully reunited with them, I almost lost my daughter due to medical complications. Shortly thereafter my mother died, a loss from which I have never quite recovered. After seven years of single parenthood, I remarried. During the next years, I had very difficult, hospital-bound pregnancies, and it was during this time that I was introduced to my husband's extreme and frightening bouts of anger. It may be hard to understand why I didn't leave him during these years of physical abuse and fear, but I had been a single mother before to two children. How could I possibly raise four children on my own? Finally, one morning, after fearing for my life, I found the courage to leave him.

I tell you these things not to complain and not to have you feel sorrow or pity for me. I tell you for this: I had had a beautiful, near-perfect life. Because I was raised with a knowledge of my Father in Heaven—that He loved me and that He was aware of me—and because I had a warm, loving family, who supported and encouraged me, I was able to recognize and acknowledge the truth of the gospel when those missionaries appeared at my door. I knew what it felt like to be guided and directed by the Spirit, and I recognized it.

So often we forget that in the premortal existence we fought alongside the Savior. We knew before we came to this earth that we would be coming to obtain physical bodies and experience. We accepted all that that meant with glad hearts and eagerness.

I would hazard a guess that no person who has ever lived has done so free of suffering, heartache, sorrow, turmoil, and sheer misery. We all sometimes question, "O God, where art thou?"

Even the Prophet Joseph, who had been visited by the Father and the Son and countless other heavenly messengers, asked that question in Liberty Jail. It was the Lord's response to Joseph at this time that brought me great comfort and even joy during my own misery: "The Son of Man hath descended below them all. Art thou greater than he?" (D&C 122:8).

Of course I knew I wasn't! Our Heavenly Father knows we learn and grow and become stronger as we face challenges and strive to overcome them. There will be times when we experience heartbreaking misery and feel we are being taken to our very limits. However, such times allow us to evolve into something different than what we were, better than we were, more empathetic, more understanding, with stronger testimonies than we had before. I know if it were not for my difficulties to overcome such heartbreak, I would have remained as I was, with little or no spiritual refinement, no progress toward my ultimate goal. I can be certain in the knowledge that my Savior knows the depths of my despair, for He has felt my every pain, my every heartache, my every anguish before me. Because of this, He alone could heal my tortured soul by encircling me about "eternally in the arms of His love"(2 Nephi 1:15).

Sooner or later, we all experience times when our entire worlds are torn apart, when we feel battered, bruised, and broken. No one is immune. All of the circumstances and details may be unique to us, but our saving grace throughout it all is the same: we can be grateful.

Despite the difficulties and uncertainties in my life, despite the heartache and pain, despite the abuse and torture, there has always been a tender, sweet peacefulness within my soul. I have known my Father loves me. I have known no parent would allow His precious child to endure that kind of anguish unless there was a greater blessing waiting at the other end. I have had gratitude for a sure knowledge that if I could see my circumstances from the vantage point of my eternal future, I would see the value and purpose for my suffering.

Such gratitude gave me the courage to become rededicated, striving with increased diligence to wax strong in the gospel, to have the Holy Ghost as my companion, and to realize my power to do all things, growing in my understanding of His principles to accomplish His plan for me. It gave me the knowledge and strength to "be still and know that [He is] God" (Psalms 46:10).

Even in my darkest moments, I knew He loved me. Then, in fact, more

> than ever, I could feel the warmth and peace of His love. In my pain, I gloried in the gratitude that I felt for my Savior's atoning sacrifice and His warm embrace. It was an honor and privilege never to be taken lightly; the Lord had found me worthy to come to this earth; He knew I was equal to the task.
>
> Numerous times during those difficult years, I asked myself, "Shall I falter, or shall I finish?"
>
> I knew I would finish!
>
> I testify to you, we have a Heavenly Father who loves us. He knows us each by name. He knows our every heartache, our every anguish, our every sorrow, for He has felt them before us. We have a Savior, even Jesus Christ, who took upon Himself the ultimate sacrifice because of His love for His Father and for us.

I testify that if we hold fast to what we know to be true and realize and accept each and every day that there is much to be grateful for, we will see things with eyes of faith. We have the blessing and knowledge of the restored gospel of the Lord Jesus Christ. That gratitude is the catalyst for all else. It is that gratitude that saved me throughout all of my adversity. This trying and also telling experience teaches us that when we are hurting the most, we feel more drastically the enabling power of the Atonement, and our gratitude for the goodness of God swells within our souls. Since all of us will have our share of adversity during this life, it is important to realize how many people are rising above their trials on a daily basis with gratitude to Heavenly Father and to feel the empowering nature of gratitude.

Chapter 2

THE EMPOWERING NATURE OF GRATITUDE

The Results of Living with and Expressing Gratitude

It is clear that the Lord knows the importance of gratitude in helping us not only keep the commandments but also be empowered to do better in our lives. There are always promised blessings within every principle and doctrine taught in the Lord's glorious gospel. Even today, modern psychology is coming to recognize the great medical benefits of gratitude, just as science realized how prophetically sound the Word of Wisdom was a generation ago. It is always reassuring when the world begins to see the light about the virtue of God's commandments.

We can learn to be grateful if we learn to see and ponder things that inspire and create feelings of gratitude and thanksgiving. There are moments when we are simply engulfed in gratitude as well as a sense of indebtedness and a desire to reciprocate goodness. And there are times when we *express* gratitude, which blesses not only the receiver but also us as the giver too.

It is interesting to note the effect gratitude has on us. In a study Robert Emmons from the University of California at Davis and Michael McCollough of Southern Methodist University in Dallas, Texas, published, we can see the difference gratitude makes in our lives.

These researchers did three separate studies of a few hundred people, in which each participant was assigned one of three tasks: to record their troubles, to record what they were grateful for, or to record life's events from a neutral standpoint. The first study had them all keep a weekly record. The second had them keep a daily journal. And the third measured only those persons with neuromuscular disease.

Each participant recorded their feelings, their moods, their behavior, and how they coped with different symptoms and behavior, including their overall evaluation of life. The results were amazing. All three studies demonstrated that the gratitude-focused groups exhibited a heightened sense of well-being. They experienced some of the following changes in their lives:

- Experienced greater levels of happiness
- Felt better about their lives as a whole
- Were more likely to help and assist others
- Were filled with hope about the future
- Experienced less illness
- Had more vitality and focus
- Made greater progress in achieving their personal goals
- Slept better
- Felt stronger during difficult times
- Enjoyed closer relationships
- Handled stress better

(See Robert A. Emmons and Michael E. McCullough, "Counting Blessings Versus Burdens: An Experimental Investigation of Gratitude and Subjective Well-Being in Daily Life," *Journal of Personality and Social Psychology* 84, no. 2 [2003]: 377–389.)

This study verifies our feelings about the inspiring nature of gratitude. The prophets and leaders have stated the importance of the commandment to thank God in all things and the empowering nature of gratitude.

Elder James E. Talmage once observed that "God requires thanksgiving, praise and worship, not for His gratification as the recipient of adulation, but for the good of His children" (*Sunday Night Talks*, 2nd ed. [Salt Lake City, Utah: The Church of Jesus Christ of Latter-day Saints, 1931], 486).

President Joseph F. Smith taught, "The grateful man sees so much in the world to be thankful for, and with him the good outweighs the evil. . . . Pride destroys our gratitude and sets up selfishness in its place" (*Gospel Doctrine, 5th ed.* [Salt Lake City: The Church of Jesus Christ of Latter-day Saints, 1939], 263).

President Thomas S. Monson encourages us to have a grateful heart:

> A grateful heart . . . comes through expressing gratitude to our Heavenly Father for His blessings and to those around us for all that they bring into our lives. This requires conscious effort—at

least until we have truly learned and cultivated an attitude of gratitude. . . .

When we encounter challenges and problems in our lives, it is often difficult for us to focus on our blessings. However, if we reach deep enough and look hard enough, we will be able to

> *Being grateful in our circumstances is an act of faith in God.*

feel and recognize just how much we have been given. . . . My brothers and sisters, to express gratitude is gracious and honorable, to enact gratitude is generous and noble, but to live with gratitude ever in our hearts is to touch heaven. ("The Divine Gift of Gratitude," *Ensign*, November 2010)

As President Dieter F. Uchtdorf has also taught, "Being grateful *in* our circumstances is an act of faith in God. It requires that we trust God and hope for things we may not see but which are true. By being grateful, we follow the example of our beloved Savior, who said, 'Not my will, but thine, be done.' True gratitude is an expression of hope *and* testimony. It comes from acknowledging that we do not always understand the trials of life but trusting that one day we will" ("Grateful in Any Circumstance," *Ensign*, May 2014).

Gratitude is not just something we do, but something we *become*.

As the aforementioned experiment revealed, the successful group was able to accept the assignment to look for the good and record their feelings of gratitude. They kept a gratitude journal. They were proactive and took action on positive events rather than being negative and acted upon. They nurtured the virtue of gratitude just like we nurture the word of God. As Alma taught us, "But if ye will nourish the word, yea, nourish the tree as it beginneth to grow, by your faith with great diligence, and with patience, looking forward to the fruit thereof, it shall take root; and behold it shall be a tree springing up unto everlasting life" (Alma 32:41). The unsuccessful groups, by contrast, looked for the negative. They recorded the events and were focused on the undesirable aspects of life or were simply neutral in their observations and actions. Or, in other words, the unsuccessful groups were *not* anxiously engaged in a good cause. The Lord's counsel of being anxiously engaged in a good cause of your own free will surely applies (see D&C 58:27–28).

The study's results speak for themselves. We've read the empirical proof—those with an attitude of gratitude, who looked for things to be grateful for and then recorded their feelings, had a dynamic change in their lives. When we live the doctrine, we will receive the blessing associated with it, the amazing changes we can experience in our lives through gratitude's transcending power.

The Kylee Schraft Story—A Lesson in Gratitude

I am so inspired by others' stories of gratitude, especially those that come from difficult trials. I was blessed to meet one such inspiration, and she has graciously allowed me to share her story with you. Kylee Schraft is a vivacious, energetic young woman. Always an avid snowboarder and lover of all things outdoors, her world would change forever one cold, snowy day in February 2012.

Kylee and a friend were overjoyed to spend a day snowboarding at Brighton Ski Resort in central Utah. They were undaunted by the heavy snow, and they were determined to get the most out of their passes and stay until the resort closed. The powder was thick, but as the evening wore on, the snow became icier with each run. Kylee and her friend were flying down the hills, feeling alive, potential frostbite seeming a small price to pay for such uninhibited joy. Although she couldn't see well through her snow-covered goggles, Kylee noticed a jump ahead and decided to go for it. She hit it hard and went sailing through the frozen air, much higher than she'd anticipated.

Gravity pulled her from her flight, and when she hit the hard-packed snow with a sickening thud, Kylee felt an incredible pain unlike anything she'd felt before shoot through her legs and toes. Screaming in agony, she tried with all her strength to move her legs. They would not move. In that moment, Kylee felt fear cut through her excruciating pain. Ski patrol transported her down the mountain, and she was Life-Flighted to the nearest hospital. Kylee believed she would die from the pain, and it wasn't until they arrived at the hospital that the medicine mercifully knocked her out.

With a broken back and other complications, Kylee hovered between life and death those first two days. Between tests and attempts to stabilize her, doctors would come in and ask Kylee to wiggle her toes. Kylee would obediently wiggle them. After about a week of this, she asked one of the doctors why she could wiggle her toes but nothing else. The doctor lifted her leg so Kylee could see her toes and said, "Wiggle." Kylee wiggled them—at least, she could feel them wiggling in her mind—but her toes didn't move at all. She was horrified as she processed this new reality. Although still experiencing indescribable pain in her back, she had absolutely no feeling whatsoever in her legs and feet. She was paralyzed from the hips down. Kylee said, "The moments in that first week were miserable in ways I cannot explain. I just cannot explain the pain and sorrow I felt." There were dark moments when she

When life gets dark and dreary, finding reasons to be grateful can be the key that unlocks the gate to light everlasting.

wished she would have died. There was constant pain, no ability to move her legs, and no hope. On a particularly bad night, Kylee cried and asked her father for a priesthood blessing. Immediately after her dad said amen, Kylee felt a change. She felt relief and hope for the first time, and this blessing became a miracle moment for Kylee.

Eventually Kylee was moved out of the ICU, but this healthy, active college student had huge hurdles yet to face. It was during the weeks she spent in her hospital room that she started feeling angry. She wondered, *Why did God put me through this? Why me? Why not someone else*? "I was so selfish and ungrateful," she said of that difficult time. "I didn't talk to people much at first, because I didn't want to talk about the condition I was in. I had always been the girl who no one told not to do something because I was going to do it anyway. I was the girl who was constantly playing sports and four-wheeling, camping, horseback riding, snowboarding, and off-roading. That was who I was. It hit me that I would never be able to be that Kylee again."

Over time, though, Kylee started to recognize all of the love and support she was receiving from her family and friends. She realized that in order to get through this, she had to be positive. She had to be the fighter she had always been. She had to have faith and be as strong as she could. She began saying, "I am in God's hands now."

As doctor after doctor told her she would be in a wheelchair permanently, she just couldn't connect to that reality. The determination, motivation, and competitive spirit that had served her so well as an athlete kept her going, and she decided she would prove those doctors wrong—that even if it took months or years, she would walk again.

Learning to walk never got easy. Even one step seemed impossibly out of Kylee's reach. Weeks turned into months, and pain remained her constant companion. Priesthood blessings of hope and courage helped keep her going. It was so challenging to have the smallest, easiest things that she had always taken for granted become the hardest things for her to do.

"Most everyone is so ungrateful for what they can do," she said. "I for sure know I was very ungrateful until the day of my accident. Imagine having to ask for help to get to the sink to brush your teeth. Imagine having to have help to use the bathroom every single time. Imagine sitting in a chair but you can't get up because your legs will not work no matter how much you want them to. Imagine looking down and knowing no matter how independent you are that you just can't do anything without asking for help. My accident caused me to lie in my hospital bed, wishing for just one step. That's all I wanted—just one, simple step!"

After months of hard work, she was finally able to take that step and then another . . . until now, two years later, she is walking, driving, and even hiking again. She has even started working in her beloved mountains as a zip line operator up the canyon. Kylee doesn't take a single moment of it for granted. "I sure do know it took an accident like this to make me realize how blessed I am. I cannot express how grateful I am for all the people who prayed for me and helped our family. Before my accident, I knew there were miracles, but I had never really witnessed one. I know I've been a part of the biggest miracle I'll probably ever experience. It took all my strength and a lot of faith to stand up and be able to take that step. I'm extremely grateful for everything I can do now. I'm especially grateful I can use the bathroom by myself again. I'm even thankful for the bursts of pain that shoot down my legs. I know that doesn't sound right, but trust me, pain is a lot better than no feeling at all! To my legs, I promise I will never call you Dumb and Dumber again! Since my accident, I live every day enjoying life because it only takes a second for it to go away."

Kylee is living proof that when we live a grateful life, even when faced with seemingly impossible challenges, we can experience incredible joy and happiness. When our minds are focused on the good and the blessings associated with it, we become new creatures. Because of her situation, Kylee was able to feel gratitude for even the smallest of things we usually take for granted. The gratitude journal can help us focus our minds in such a manner. When we express, record, and ponder those things we are grateful for, we will feel a sense of joy and happiness, the by-products of a grateful heart. Start counting your blessings daily and recording them, and watch how you change.

You will notice how the day will seem brighter. A joyous and happy countenance will fill you. Like Alma said, experiment upon my words. Trust me on this one—you won't believe how happy you will become!

Journaling Moment of Joy

Take a moment to think of some wonderful things in your life. Think of some of the small, everyday miracles you experience. Now put them in your journal and watch what happens to your whole outlook. It's magical. If you sow good thoughts, you reap good feelings.

Gratitude Lessons from Our Prophets and Leaders

President David O. McKay taught us an empowering truth about happiness:

> Happiness consists not of having, but of being; not of possessing, but of enjoying. It is a warm glow of the heart at peace with itself. A martyr at the stake may have happiness that a king on his throne might envy. Man is the creator

> of his own happiness. It is the aroma of life, lived in harmony with high ideals. For what a man *has* he may be dependent upon others; what he *is* rests with him alone. What he *obtains* in life is but acquisition; what he *attains* is true growth. (David O. McKay, *Pathways to Happiness* [Salt Lake City: Deseret Book Company, 1957], 104)

Note how we can swap out happiness for gratitude in every instance in the preceding statement, and it will read exactly the same! That is not an accident: happiness is a part of gratitude, and gratitude is part of happiness. They go hand in hand.

Furthermore, gratitude is also part of what helps us lay hold of the Atonement: Christ empowers us through His infinite Atonement when we receive and accept it into our hearts with gratitude. Now, the receiver must accept from the giver with a grateful heart so both can be edified and uplifted, "for what doth it profit a man if a gift [the love of God] is bestowed upon him, and he receive not the gift? Behold, he rejoices not in that which is given unto him, neither rejoices in him who is the giver of the gift" (D&C 88:33). The Lord's joy lies in our receiving His Atonement, as does our joy.

President Howard W. Hunter gave us insight into the joy of gratitude when he said, "Gratitude *is a spiritual attribute.* One of the most esteemed spiritual attributes we can acquire in life is sincere gratitude. It enriches our lives as we, through this attribute, enrich the lives of others. If we have a thankful heart we will have the blessings that come from constant appreciation for the things done for us and the Lord's goodness. . . . Happiness and joy from blessings are never complete until there is a deep feeling of gratitude within oneself which moves an expression of appreciation" (*The Teachings of Howard W. Hunter* [Salt Lake City: Bookcraft, 1997], 92–93).

President Dieter F. Uchtdorf reminds us, "Everyone's situation is different, and the details of each life are unique. Nevertheless, I have learned that there is something that would take away the bitterness that may come into our lives.

There is one thing we can do to make life sweeter, more joyful, even glorious. We can be grateful!" ("Grateful in Any Circumstances," *Ensign*, May 2014).

President Gordon B. Hinckley has taught, "Our society is afflicted by a spirit of thoughtless arrogance unbecoming those who have been so magnificently blessed. How grateful we should be for the bounties we enjoy. Absence of gratitude is the mark of the narrow, uneducated mind. It bespeaks a lack of knowledge and the ignorance of self-sufficiency. It expresses itself in ugly egotism and frequently in wanton mischief. . . . Where there is appreciation, there is courtesy, there is concern for the rights and property of others. Without appreciation, there is arrogance and evil. Where there is gratitude, there is humility, as opposed to pride" ("'With All Thy Getting Get Understanding,'" *Ensign*, August 1988).

Consider the following quote by Elder Joseph B. Wirthlin:

> Gratitude is a mark of a noble soul and a refined character. We like to be

> around those who are grateful. They tend to brighten all around them. They make others feel better about themselves. They tend to be more humble, more joyful, more likable. . . . In the Book of Mormon we learn that we should "live in thanksgiving daily" (Alma 34:38). Isn't that a wonderful thought to live in thanksgiving daily? Can you imagine how your life would improve if you lived in thanksgiving daily? Can you imagine how your life would improve if others did the same? Do you think the world would be a happier place? less stressful? less angry? more spiritual? ("Live in Thanksgiving Daily," *Ensign*, September 2001)

Journaling Moment of Joy

Think of someone you really enjoy being around. In your gratitude journal, list a few of the qualities that person has that you admire. How do these qualities contribute to an attitude of gratitude?

Gratitude Is Self-Perpetuating and Enhanced with Praise and Encouragement

Gratitude is self-perpetuating. It is contagious. It is synergistic. Everyone who is around gratitude and thanksgiving feels better.

Some neuroscientists have declared that the reward center in the brain is actually stimulated when we're feeling grateful. Amazing! And why shouldn't it? We feel good when we receive appreciation and gratitude, and we feel good when we give it. This is why praise is one of the most dominant influences to change. Praise fosters gratitude and unleashes the power within. People change when they are given thanks and are continually reinforced to do better. Let me share an example of the empowering force of gratitude from my own life:

One day when I was in high school, the new basketball coach, Don Snow, called me into his office and said, "Ed, I've been watching you, and with a few small changes, you are going to be great. I'll show you how. You will be my starting center and captain of the team."

Something immediately sparked in my heart, and my game quickly improved. I was not only excited, but I was also enthused about my future. That year our team took second place in the state tournament, I was voted All-State, I led the region in scoring, and, in the end, I was offered a BYU scholarship to play ball for the legendary coach Stan Watts.

I had great success and wonderful victories playing college basketball, and it all started with a person I admired saying "You are going to be great." My improvement came in large part as the product of a great coach who gave me praise and encouragement, and for that I am eternally grateful.

We could even make a little acronym for praising people. Give them PIE every day: **P**raise, **I**nspiration, **E**ncouragement. As you care for others, PIE will become a natural expression of your concern and compassion for them. Giving people PIE motivates them to greater heights. The Holy Spirit will guide you and give you the words you need to say. This way your PIE will always be genuine and heartfelt. You'll be like Nephi, who said, "And I was led by the Spirit, not knowing beforehand the things which I should do" (1 Nephi 4:6). The Holy Spirit "will show unto you all things what ye should do" (2 Nephi 32:5).

Journaling Moment of Joy

In your gratitude journal, write the name of someone who could use a little PIE today (everyone could). Think of a specific way to praise them, inspire them, or encourage them, and commit to share it with them sometime this week. After you've shared some PIE, take a moment to write how it made you feel. Processing this moment increases the capacity of your grateful heart.

A grateful person is more likely to bless others' lives through genuine encouragement and praise. Some of the greatest blessings in life lie in the expression of approval for something someone else has done. People need approval. People need to feel accepted. People need to know they are all right. People need to know they are of worth and can do meaningful things. "The deepest principle in human nature is the craving to be appreciated," an American psychologist and philosopher William James

(1842–1910) said. Genuine praise becomes one of the greatest motivating tools in the world. Say something good about your family, friends, and coworkers. It will bless your life as well as theirs.

We probably have no idea how many people in our lives would suddenly blossom if we gave them more genuine praise. And we would be deeply impressed with the results.

Change is a compliment away for the giver and receiver when they are filled with gratitude. They become more optimistic about the future because gratitude increases their hope, thus enabling optimism to envelop their very being.

Helping Others Is a Natural Consequence of Gratitude.

Gratitude is like a well-formed muscle-use it or lose it.

Sister Sheri L. Dew recognized the magnificent motivating power of gratitude when she said, "If for nothing else than an expression of gratitude for the Savior's resplendent gift, can we help and care for each other? Imagine the cumulative, magnifying, multiplying effect if each one of us helped strengthen just one or two others during the next twelve months. It would be impossible to measure the influence—for those we help, and for us as well" (Sheri L. Dew, *No Doubt About It* [Salt Lake City: Bookcraft, 2001], 77).

When we write and express our feelings of gratitude, our hearts are not only touched but also unlocked and become full of compassion. We care about others. In caring, we seek to serve and bless them in any manner possible. Love is unleashed, for love is that ultimate concern that brings about righteous service. I observed this phenomenon firsthand while serving as a mission president in England. The missionaries would write me a weekly letter, and they were so good and so kind. These are the words I would read on a regular basis: "Oh, president, this week has been wonderful. Our convert, Susan, was baptized. The change that has occurred in her life has been wonderful. I have never been so happy in all my life."

Unbeknownst to them, they were keeping a gratitude journal of sorts for me and were feeling that empowering influence by doing so. Their joy had swallowed up all of their hardships as gratitude encompassed their very being. Alma said, "I glory in that which the Lord hath commanded me; yea, and this is my glory, that perhaps I may be an instrument in the hands of God to bring some soul to repentance; and this is my joy. And behold, when I see many of my brethren truly penitent, and coming to the Lord their God, then is my soul filled with joy; then do I remember what the Lord has done for me, yea, even that he hath heard my prayer; yea, then do I remember his merciful arm which he extended towards me" (Alma 29:9–10).

Notice how when Alma is filled with joy, he immediately (because of a grateful heart) remembers all the Lord has done for him. The Lord has heard his prayers, and His merciful arm is extended to Alma. Gratitude is empowering because when your heart is full of gratitude, you feel reenergized to continue in the path of righteousness.

Gratitude reinforces behavior. It motivates and increases our capacity to do good. I have watched my children, my students, and my missionaries respond to expressions of gratitude and thanksgiving. "Thanks for helping. You are terrific." They redoubled their efforts to be more helpful. "Thanks for cleaning up after the dance." They were there for cleanup after every dance. When I praised one missionary with, "I am so grateful for the way you serve the Lord with all your heart," the following week he said, "President, I have this great idea. If we get up at 4:30, we can be at the bus stop and talk to three times as many people at 7:30 rather than at 9:30 when we usually get there. Isn't that great? We will let you know how it goes." I literally had to encourage this companionship to be careful to not overdo it in their proselyting efforts. They were so devoted. My eyes still well up with tears when I think of the Lord's missionaries I had the honor of serving with. They were diligent, dedicated, and relentless in helping others come unto Christ. I never praised them or expressed gratitude with the hopes of inspiring greater effort; I learned these things after I experienced them. If you express gratitude in order to manipulate, you will reap the whirlwinds of deceit. A grateful heart inspires one to express gratitude as a natural response. The increased motivation the receiver of your praise feels is just a wonderful side effect.

Journaling Moment of Joy

The record of your gratitude journal will be engraved in your heart. And your grandchildren will be inspired when they read it one day. Take a minute to write them a message of PIE. Long after you are gone, your grateful heart will bless your posterity.

Live in Thanksgiving Daily

The Lord revealed to Joseph Smith, "And he who receiveth all things with thankfulness shall be made glorious" (D&C 78:19). We have more enthusiasm, are filled with the Holy Spirit, and have a greater desire to do good as we are grateful.

Our prayers are more meaningful. In gratitude we are able to focus more as we ponder and pray to our Heavenly Father. Indeed, gratitude is self-generating. This is why we have more energy, enthusiasm, and focus when we are thankful and invite the Spirit into our lives.

I have experienced this so many times. I am at a stage in life that some call the "twilight years." Some tell me to slow down, but I feel energized and more focused than ever. I want to do more and do better. As an example, all I have to do is think of how grateful I am for my family, and I feel inspired to do family history work. I get help from various Church resources, but I also get special help from my granddaughter Emily, who not only assists me but also sets an example for the whole family to do family history. Making progress on doing this important work for my family fills me with even more gratitude, which is empowering and produces more energy and enthusiasm—a wonderful cycle of energized gratitude and productivity.

Journaling Moment of Joy

Take a moment to ponder the sacrament prayer found in D&C 20:77. What happened to your gratitude for your beloved Savior? Record those feelings. Taking the time to let gratitude fill your heart brings a multiplicity of blessings here and now.

Doing Good Creates a Grateful Heart

My amazing young friend Britner Mecham, at twelve years old, has eloquently shared his thoughts with me about his goal of attending the temple and doing family history: "Going to the temple is like eating your favorite food, except not with your physical body but with your spiritual body. When you eat your favorite food, you can't help but be grateful that you got it, and you want more of it. Brigham Young's daughter, Susa Young, once asked how we would get the great amount of temple work that needed to be done finished. Brigham then told her there will be many timesaving devices that will allow people to make time to go to the temple. When you go to the temple, you feel a feeling of peace and gratitude. I get those same feelings when I do family history work. When I get those feelings of gratitude, I want to get them more and more. This keeps me focused on doing my family history research."

Britner also said, "Doing FamilySearch and indexing is a great motivator to get you to the temple. Not only do you feel successful when you find family names, but you also want to go to the temple and do the temple work. When I can't find names, I am so grateful that I can pray to Father in Heaven and that He will help me. Indexing is also really cool. Not only are you doing the Lord's work, but you are helping other people do their family history work too. FamilySearch is amazing; my little brother and I have helped my mom get the true meaning of Elder Scott's promised blessings of temple work using family names. My whole life she has gone to the temple weekly, but before 2013, she had never taken a family name. We are so grateful that we can find our ancestors and do this life-saving work for them. I really love to do family history work because I feel good inside and grateful for my blessings." Doing good creates a grateful heart.

Gratitude Can Turn Night into Day

We have all had dark days when we've felt like there was no way out or up.

On one such day, I was encountering a problem with no quick turnaround or solution. I could not feel hope but rather was only thinking about my problem and myself. I couldn't understand how or why it had happened. I struggled emotionally and spiritually so much that I couldn't think of anything uplifting. Then, through much pleading and prayer, I finally got hold of myself. I thought of my blessings and of how much worse the situation could be. Through gratitude and thanksgiving, I felt as though the Savior had wrapped his loving arms around me. I realized how blessed I was and how much hope I had because of the enabling power of the Atonement and the comfort of the Holy Ghost. There *was* hope to carry on. Gratitude for the goodness and mercy of God carried me through. Now I marvel at how this overwhelming challenge made it possible for me to help others. Strange but true! Everything we experience can make us into better sons and daughters of God, better instruments in His hands. Indeed, we will have more holiness through gratitude.

It is trying times that bring about our greatest growth, as Sister Sheri L. Dew has taught:

> During the recent past, I have faced a baffling challenge that has tested my faith and my spiritual mettle all over again. I've worked and fasted and pleaded for help. But the answers haven't come easily or quickly. At times things have looked hopeless—until I have asked myself one question: "Sheri, do you believe the Lord will help you, or don't you?"
>
> That question always stops me short. Because I do believe. I believe He will help because He always has. He hasn't always given me everything I've prayed for—far from it—but He has never let me down. He always helps me and gives me what I need. And every time I undergo another divine tutorial, it increases my reservoir of faith for the next challenge. As hard as it is, I am grateful every time my faith is

stretched, because *only* if our testimony of Jesus Christ penetrates every aspect of our lives will we be able to do what we have come here to do. (Sheri L. Dew, *No One Can Take Your Place* [Salt Lake City: Deseret Book Company, 2004], 15–16).

 **Journaling Moment of Joy**

Gratitude is our panacea for life.

Isn't it fun to stop every once in a while and make an entry in your gratitude journal? When life is at its worst, the panacea is the love of God, and gratitude for that love can carry you through tenuous times. You realize things could be worse. Look for the good and preserve those thoughts in your gratitude journal.

Expressing Gratitude Deepens Relationships

When gratitude and appreciation are expressed

to our loved ones, our interpersonal relationships are better in every way. They are deeper, stronger, and longer lasting. In the marriage relationship, showing and expressing appreciation is vital to keeping romance alive and commitment strong. Through continual displays of gratitude, your love will be ongoing and bring joy to your partner. Remember that to be loved and appreciated is every human being's greatest need.

There is something about giving and receiving a compliment and expressing thanksgiving that not only arouses gratitude within our whole souls but also enhances our relationships at the same time. When we feel gratitude for someone, the bond of love is increased. Each time an expression of love is received, that relationship is deepened, and both parties feel reciprocal gratitude. In other words, whenever we are grateful to another person, our relationship is strengthened.

This has been evident in my own life and especially in my marriage. My sweetheart, Pat, has written the following about expressing gratitude in a relationship:

I've found that expressed gratitude brings increased love to both the giver and the receiver and, most importantly, deepens our relationship and strengthens our bonds.

I love color. The spring and summer flowers in all of their stunning colors bring such joy to my heart and such gratitude and love for my Heavenly Father and Savior. Of course, I also love the fall leaves and the crisp blue sky on a white winter day.

This is a beautiful earth, a beautiful place to live, and when I remember that our Father and Savior created it just for us, I am so grateful, and my heart is filled with such love for Them.

I enjoy bringing color into our home. I try to do that with pillows. You might say I have a fetish for brightly colored pillows. My sweetheart, Ed, laughs about our storeroom that has shelves and shelves of pillows. He is such a good sport.

> Our home is mostly off-white—the tile, walls, and couches—so each season of the year, I bring out the appropriate pillows and colored glass vases and flowers to honor that season. I use a lot of red because in our senior years it is too difficult to change the area rug with each season, and it is a deep red. In the winter, I use reds and purples; in the spring I add pink and a vase of pink and red blossoms; in the summer, yellows, greens, and reds; and in the fall, reds, orange, and gold.
>
> It never fails that Ed will notice and thank me for making our home beautiful. I love that, and I love him even more, if that's possible, when he notices and comments and thanks me. Expressing gratitude toward each other is a magical key that strengthens our relationship.

Explicitly showing gratitude and appreciation to others is part of expressing love.

Unexpressed gratitude does not qualify as gratitude because the receiver cannot acknowledge it.

Gratitude unexpressed does not fulfill the measure of its creation.

Gratitude and thanksgiving require expression and action because gratitude unexpressed does not fulfill the measure of its creation.

Just think about how you feel toward someone after they express gratitude to you for something. The blessings are self-evident. One compliment can last a long time. Continued genuine compliments reinforce past compliments and build up a reservoir of strength. It kindles a desire to maintain that compliment, as happened with my old coach and me. Gracious compliments are like positive labeling. You become better simply because that is what you are! Watch what happens when you tell a young child they are (insert any compliment here). Whatever that compliment is, they will seek to become it. Beware of false labels and negative labeling, as they can be devastating to a child or anyone else.

Journaling Moment of Joy

Compliment your sweetheart now. A hug, a call, a text message, or an e-mail expressing your gratitude will make their day.

A Grateful Heart Can Build Resilience

Gratitude can help us build a mattress of power so that when we fall, we are cushioned and have the resilience to bounce back in every situation. Gratitude is incredible! To help us in stressful situations, we can use positive self-talk. We can ask ourselves questions that will turn the moment into an empowering challenge rather than a stumbling block of disaster. Here are some examples:

Example 1: "What can I learn from this?"

Throughout my life, I have found that I learn more from difficult situations than from anything else. Often the gratitude I feel for what I learn comes later as I look back on that very difficult time.

Journaling Moment of Joy

Recall three difficult situations or trials you have experienced. What did you learn from them?

Take a moment to thank the people who have helped you. Remember, your giving PIE will feed someone for weeks. It is incredibly powerful. Tell your children and grandchildren (even possible future children) how PIE makes you feel.

As a young boy working on our farm, I was often asked by my father to go pull burdock. Burdock is a leafy plant with cockle burrs, and every time I went out to pull them, I thought to myself, *I cannot pull all of these burdock plants! There are thousands of them on the farm.* It was with reluctance that I would pull them because I wanted to play more than anything. I even tried to hide when I came home from school, but it seemed my dad could always find me, and I would inevitably be told to go pull burdock. Over the years, I learned that work is vital to my growth. But I was never grateful for the opportunity to obey immediately and work continuously . . . so it seemed.

Fast-forward forty years to when I was serving as president of the England London South Mission. As I was walking out of my house one day, I thought about the glorious missionaries, how hard they work and how diligently they serve, and my mind went back to my youth.

At that moment, tears welled up in my eyes, and I said a silent prayer of gratitude to my Heavenly Father. My earthly father had taught me the blessing of work and obedience from the time I was a little boy. It took forty years to be grateful and realize this—to develop eyes to see and a heart to feel gratitude for my father—but how grateful I am to have finally realized my debt of gratitude to my father for how he taught me to work and obey. Those two virtues have blessed me in every aspect of my life.

Feelings of gratitude for what we've gone through often come later through other life lessons.

Example 2: "Is there anything in this stressful challenge that can elicit feelings of thanksgiving and gratitude?"

Once gratitude gets in the way of stress, you will find that stress slowly but surely dissolves away. That is because you are turning the stressful situation around and are now in control. Stress occurs when you lack control or are not prepared for the situation.

Example 3: "Has this difficult test in my life prepared me to better deal with stress?"

If so, hallelujah! Remember that change is required for growth. If you do not change and learn to deal with stress, it will control you. With gratitude ready to carry you onward and upward, you will learn as I have that gratitude can help you overcome these fearful and challenging moments. This gratitude helps you increase your pleading prayers, have an abundance of charity and love, prepare for these moments, exercise your faith in Jesus Christ, enlarge your knowledge about how to deal with stress, and, above all, experience stress as a challenge rather than a crisis. Gratitude is a catalyst to change, and you will need a catalyst to fight through stressful times of life.

Remember That Gratitude Brings Its Own Rewards

In Alma 5, the prophet Alma asks fifty questions to inspire and provoke the people to righteousness. The first five are about remembering the goodness of God, which brought gratitude to the people. Here are the first five questions in order:

1. Have you sufficiently retained in remembrance the captivity of your fathers? (v. 6)
2. Have you sufficiently retained in remembrance His mercy and long-suffering towards them? (v. 6)
3. Have ye sufficiently retained in remembrance that He has delivered their souls from hell? (v. 6)
4. Were they destroyed? (v. 8)
5. Were the bands of death broken, and the chains of hell which encircled them about, were they loosed? (v. 9)

Gratitude always occurs when we *remember*. It is when we forget that gratitude is no longer a force for good. Whenever the Nephites forgot the goodness of God and to thank Him daily, they would become wicked: "Thus we see how quick the children of men do forget the Lord their God, yea, how quick to do iniquity, and to be led away by the evil one" (Alma 46:8).

But with gratitude toward God, we escape the pitfalls of the evil one as we instead, almost instinctively, call upon our Heavenly Father and He helps us. As the Lord Himself tells us, "If ye have faith ye can do all things which are expedient unto me" (Moroni 10:23). Gratitude is strengthening.

Journaling Moment of Joy

When you are at a low ebb and life is dreary and difficult, just stop. Go to your comfiest chair. Ponder on the goodness of God for a few minutes. Now record that in your journal, and it will be recorded in your grateful heart. Have you noticed? Life is good.

Gratitude Is a Building Block for Life

Gratitude builds togetherness and unity in families and groups. It also builds character because it shows that you have a greater capacity to appreciate the good. Your character is enlarged and radiates to those around you. Far from showing weakness and generating dependency, gratitude, if practiced on a consistent basis, helps build feelings of confidence and self-worth. Throughout my life, whether on the athletic field, making a presentation, or working on a project, I realized that if I tried hard I would be able to accomplish the task. Comments like, "Your talk was just what I needed. Thanks so much," or "Your effort down the stretch changed the game. You saved the day," made all the difference. I am more than eighty years old, and I have confidence because of the expressions of praise and gratitude that have constantly come into my life. In a very tender and personal way, I know that when I please my Heavenly Father and do His will, I feel His love and gratitude for me. Yes, expressing gratitude builds character and self-confidence.

Gratitude builds leadership skills. It affects our ability to lead as the Savior leads, as gratitude is an element of Christlike leadership that attracts others to follow our examples. Loving people is easy for me because I know who I am and my relationship to my brothers and sisters. But love can also come as tough love or chastening, which also requires a great leader to be strong.

Such was the case as I served as mission president when several elders needed some extra guidance. My stomach ached, and I didn't want to chastise them, but because I loved them and because of the commandments of the Lord and inspiration of the Holy Ghost, I knew I had to. "Verily, thus saith the Lord unto you whom I love, and whom I love I also chasten that their sins may be forgiven, for with the chastisement I prepare a way for their deliverance in all things out of temptation, and I have loved you" (D&C 95:1). And again the Lord has said, "Reproving betimes with sharpness, when moved upon by the Holy Ghost; and then showing forth afterwards an increase of love toward him whom thou hast reproved, lest he esteem thee to be his enemy" (D&C 121:43).

After a lengthy prayer prior to meeting with these elders, I explained to them, one at a time, with gentleness and meekness, how much I loved them and cared for them. I then explained that their behavior was not pleasing to Heavenly Father and our Savior. I could not hold back the tears. We embraced, and I felt so much love for each young man. To my surprise and joy, their expressions of gratitude were forthcoming at that moment and throughout the rest of their time on their missions. These elders could tell how hard it was for me to do what I knew I had to do. They knew it was for their good, and our bond was deepened and secured. Love and gratitude for each other forged that bond that would not be broken. They would follow, and I could lead; we were happy, and the Lord was pleased.

Gratitude is related to the fruits of the Holy Spirit and cannot be commanded or demanded; it must come forth from the depths of our hearts.

Gratitude Brings the Blessings of the Spirit

Perhaps the greatest of all rewards for a grateful heart is the blessing of the Spirit. We often feel this blessing of the Spirit as we express or receive gratitude because true gratitude comes to us through the Spirit: "Love, joy, peace, longsuffering, gentleness, goodness, faith, meekness, temperance: against such there is no law" (Galatians 5:22–23).

Again, we learn: "And now, verily, verily, I say unto thee, put your trust in that Spirit which leadeth to do good—yea, to do justly, to walk humbly, to judge righteously; and this is my Spirit. Verily, verily, I say unto you, I will impart unto you of my Spirit, which shall enlighten your mind, which shall fill your soul with joy; And then shall ye know, or by this shall you know, all things whatsoever you desire of me, which are pertaining unto things of righteousness, in faith believing in me that you shall receive" (D&C 11:12–14).

The surest way, then, to know if gratitude will improve all aspects of your life is to put your trust in the Spirit, who leads you to be grateful.

Some of the first things we feel when we experience gratitude are gladness, satisfaction, pleasure, serenity, and gratification. Gratitude is so empowering that our lives feel more significant, with more depth and meaning, and our spirituality is definitely increased. The end result of feeling grateful and expressing gratitude is peace and love. We find true joy and happiness as gratitude finds a way into our heart and to all the hearts we touch.

Chapter 3

THE BIRTH AND BEGINNING OF THE VIRTUE OF GRATITUDE

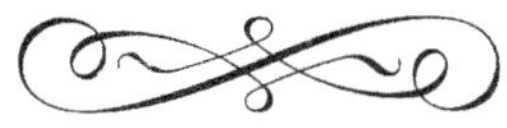

If you worry that you are not possessed of gratitude just yet, fret not: the development of gratitude within our souls is a process. The seed of gratitude lives within every living soul's heart, but it must undergo a germination process, where we and the enabling power of the Atonement nurture the seed. Through a series of good practices, such as praying for a grateful heart,

> *Your life is a result of your attitudes and actions. When gratitude is your attitude and love is the motivation of your actions, life will be abundant and full of joy.*

looking for the good in everything, recording in a journal those things we are grateful for, and having an attitude of gratitude, our gratitude comes alive and grows and matures into a tree—a tree of empowerment, a tree of life.

The tree of gratitude produces life-giving fruit that changes our perspective and enhances our vision of life. Our eyes and ears, our hearts, and our very souls become different as we see the good around us, even when good is hard to find. We become new people as virtues stream into our lives because of gratitude's empowerment. As Melody Beattie, a self-help expert, said, "Gratitude unlocks the fullness of life. It turns what we have into enough, and more. It turns denial into acceptance, chaos to order, confusion to clarity. It can turn a meal into a feast, a house into a home, a stranger into a friend. . . . Gratitude makes sense of our past, brings peace for today, and creates a vision for tomorrow" (Melody Beattie, *The Language of Letting Go* [Center City, Minnesota: Hazelden, 1990], 218).

Just thinking of this statement makes me want to increase my gratitude for all things. Former

Relief Society General President Bonnie D. Parkin has also given wonderful insights into gratitude. She said, "Gratitude is a Spirit-filled principle. It opens our minds to a universe permeated with the richness of a living God. Through it, we become spiritually aware of the wonder of the smallest things, which gladden our hearts with their messages of God's love. This grateful awareness heightens our sensitivity to divine direction. When we communicate gratitude, we can be filled with the Spirit and connected to those around us and the Lord. Gratitude inspires happiness and carries divine influence. 'Live in thanksgiving daily,' said Amulek, 'for the many mercies and blessings which he doth bestow upon you'" ("Gratitude: A Path to Happiness," *Ensign*, May 2007).

Gratitude is so important that President James E. Faust declared, "To 'thank the Lord thy God in all things' (D&C 59:7) is more than a social courtesy; it is a binding commandment" ("Gratitude as a Saving Principle," *Ensign*, December 1996).

Likewise, President Henry B. Eyring has said:

> Our Father in Heaven commands us to be thankful in all things (see 1 Thessalonians 5:18), and He requires that we give thanks for the blessings we receive (see D&C 46:32). We know that all of His commandments are intended to make us happy, and we also know that to break commandments leads to misery. So to be happy and to avoid misery, we must have a grateful heart. We have seen in our lives the connection between gratitude and happiness. All of us would like to feel gratitude, yet it is not easy to be consistently grateful in all things in the trials of life. Sickness, disappointment, and the loss of people we love come at times in our lives. Our sorrows can make it hard to see our blessings and to appreciate the blessings God has in store for us in the future. ("The Choice to Be Grateful," *Ensign*, December 2011)

It is easy to talk about being grateful but not always easy to actually *feel* grateful. So how do we do it? How do we change the inner vessel? How does our heart become a grateful heart?

We Can Learn to Express Gratitude in a Sensitive and Sincere Manner Every Day

Becoming an authentic person free of guile or deception takes time. It is a process of becoming. When President David O. McKay was a young missionary, there was a time when, like most missionaries, he was struggling a bit. One afternoon he passed a building where the stone above the door had a carved inscription of a quotation, supposedly from Shakespeare, which read, "What-E'er Thou Art, Act Well Thy Part." Upon reading those words, President McKay had the following experience:

> I said to myself, or the Spirit within me, "You are a member of the Church of Jesus Christ of Latter-day Saints. More than that, you are here as a representative of the Lord Jesus Christ. You accepted the responsibility as a representative of the Church." Then I thought [about] what we had done that

> forenoon. We had been sightseeing; we had gained historical instruction and information, it is true, and I was thrilled with it. . . . However, that was not missionary work. . . . I accepted the message given to me on that stone, and from that moment we tried to do our part as missionaries in Scotland. (Francis M. Gibbons, *David O. McKay: Apostle to the World, Prophet of God* [Salt Lake City: Deseret Book Company, 1986], 45)

That stone is now in the Provo MTC foyer and was placed there to inspire the missionaries when I was serving there in 1989.

The principle of acting as if we possess a quality or character attribute becomes a way in which we can begin to become a person with a pure and grateful heart. We choose to express gratitude with tenderness and love, with a sensitive and sincere manner, and with meekness. We can express gratitude even when we're not feeling 100 percent grateful. We think in our hearts, and we become what we think (see Proverbs 23:7).

As in all things, the Holy Spirit will assist us in speaking words of gratitude because we care, "for it shall be given you in the very hour, yea, in the very moment, what ye shall say" (D&C 100:6). We simply practice expressing gratitude.

How Do We Feel and Share Gratitude in Trying Moments?

While serving our mission with our family in England, we had an occasion to attend a youth fireside at the Hyde Park chapel. President Thomas S. Monson, a counselor in the First Presidency at the time, was to speak. Prior to the meeting, we gathered for a prayer upstairs with Wendell Ashton, the president of the London mission; President Monson; and our families. As we were visiting before the prayer, the phone rang, and the secretary quickly came to inform me that it was my son calling from the States. My son said, "Dad, Cory's been in a car accident. He's badly hurt, and he's in a coma." My heart sank as I told my sweetheart this news about our youngest son, who had returned to Utah to finish high school and play football his senior year. When President Monson heard what had happened, he pulled his airline ticket out of his pocket and gave it to Pat (you could do this back in 1986), and said to her, "Take this. Go to your son." He went on to tell me that if things didn't get better in two days, I would need to return home as well. Two days later, my two daughters and I returned to the States. I arrived at the hospital, where I saw Cory on life support, and my heart just broke. The outlook was very bleak. I prayed fervently to my Heavenly Father because I knew all He had to do was say yes and Cory could live. I pleaded in prayer throughout that night, but the answer I received was that Cory had to go home to Heavenly Father. My sweetheart was holding his hand as the machines were turned off and until his body turned cold. My dear son, Cory Matthew Pinegar, had returned home.

Ever the servant, President Monson called several times to get a report on Cory's condition. When hearing of Cory's passing, President Monson expressed his sorrow and asked how he might help. I asked if he would speak at his funeral, and he responded with loving-kindness, "I hoped you would ask." At the funeral, President

Monson spoke with great empathy and power. He said, "Don't ask why. That is a negative comment. He had his mission call early and is transferred to the spirit world, where a great deal of work is going on." Then he smiled and said, "I can see him with his new companion, yes, Elder LeGrand Richards—that would be a great twosome." We all smiled and laughed. It brought joy to a somber family. Then, with the power of the Melchizedek priesthood, he bestowed an apostolic blessing upon our family and spoke of how we would be healed by the enabling power of the Atonement and we would carry on serving the Lord in England.

We returned to England with the pain of a lost loved one. I felt as if my entire body had been ripped from its moorings. It seemed my entire soul was wrenched in pain. The very innards of my body and mind were racked with sorrow. Flesh of my flesh, my beloved son, with such a bright future, was dead. I felt so weakened. How could I ever preach and teach with power to inspire the missionaries? I had lost my dad when I was a little twelve-year-old boy, but this was a profoundly different experience. Was this opposition too much for me to handle? And then the miracle happened. The power of the Atonement entered my family, and the pain was swept away. There were moments of tenderness when our thoughts would turn to Cory, but we were healed. We knew he was happy serving his mission in the spirit world.

When I spoke with the missionaries the following week after our return, they were amazed. Greater power filled my soul. Inspiring words came by the power of the Holy Ghost. The Lord, in His goodness through a living prophet, had made me into something I cannot describe, except to say He had made me into an instrument to do His work. I knew whom I was serving and who was helping me at every turn. The Lord and His goodness are ever present as He succors and blesses His children.

It was in the pain of this great trial of losing a son that the supernal knowledge and power of the infinite Atonement came to me. Its enabling power was real. I felt it. I know it works. I know I was healed from my grief and sorrow. I now preach and teach with greater faith, conviction, and power, all through the goodness and mercy of God. There is a difference in my heart. I am more grateful to my Father and my Savior. I acknowledge my nothingness and rejoice in my dependence upon Their strength in my life. My empathy and compassion have increased. I am now better able to help someone who is struggling. I never would have been able to understand and appreciate their sorrow or grief if I had not known it and been healed myself. The pain of opposition was the requirement for me to suffer so I could more deeply appreciate the Atonement and my beloved son's life. Pain resolved to peace and brokenheartedness to joy. Many times it is only through suffering that we can grow.

The miracle was that Cory was alive on the other side, working diligently as a missionary, and through the expression of the priesthood, the power of the Atonement had healed my soul. There was no grief, and there was no sorrow; there was joy, for Cory had been a good boy and would be a great missionary. It was with gratitude on bended knee, with tears streaming down my cheeks, that I thanked Heavenly Father for His blessed Son Jesus Christ, who had suffered and sacrificed so we could be healed in these trying times. I am a recipient of Alma's words: "And he shall go forth, suffering pains and afflictions and temptations of every kind; and this that the word might be fulfilled which saith he will take upon him the pains and the sicknesses of his people. And he will take upon him death, that he may loose the bands of death which bind his people; and he will take upon him their infirmities, that his bowels may be filled with mercy, according to the flesh, that he may know according to the flesh how to succor his people according to their infirmities" (Alma 7:11–12).

I had been nurtured and healed because of the condescension of Christ as He performed the infinite and eternal Atonement. I felt gratitude and am still continually refreshed in my soul every time I think of my son Cory.

Once we realize gratitude can pull us out of these trying and difficult moments, it becomes easier to express our gratitude. Gratitude helps turn us around from thinking of ourselves and to opening the way for the Lord to empower us. The more trying the situation, the more we need to rely on gratitude's empowering nature.

Journaling Moment of Joy

Think about one of your difficult trials. As your mind ponders this challenge, are you able to recognize ways the Savior's Atonement has helped ease your pain and heal your heart? Take a moment and write about your feelings, drawing on the empowering nature of finding gratitude even in the hardest times.

Following the tragic auto accident that took Cory, we found ourselves deeply grateful that

> *Gratitude can take sorrow away from your heart when you joy in others' blessings.*

the passenger in the car was unharmed. It was a tender moment when we talked with her parents and expressed these feelings. Gratitude can take sorrow away from your heart when you joy in others' blessings.

In every tragic moment, gratitude can empower us through the Savior's Atonement and help ease our pain and heal our hearts. Because of our son's seemingly untimely death, we live with the hope of being together eternally. In the midst of struggle, we can thank Heavenly Father for angels who can help (see Mosiah 27:14). We look to God for help in all things, and we can be thankful for the enabling power of the Lord's infinite Atonement.

How Do We Continually Feel Gratitude in Prosperous Times?

Sometimes we are quick to remember God during times of trouble but slow to remember Him when times are good. God's children often forget Him during prosperous times.

> Yea, and we may see at the very time when he doth prosper his people, yea, in the increase of their fields, their flocks and their herds, and in gold, and

> in silver, and in all manner of precious things of every kind and art; sparing their lives, and delivering them out of the hands of their enemies; softening the hearts of their enemies that they should not declare wars against them; yea, and in fine, doing all things for the welfare and happiness of his people; yea, *then is the time that they do harden their hearts, and do forget the Lord their God, and do trample under their feet the Holy One—yea, and this because of their ease, and their exceedingly great prosperity.* (Helaman 12:2, emphasis added)

When we are struggling, our prayers are more pleading out of desperation. When all is well, we often fail to seek help at all because we supposedly have everything we need—a big mistake. Fixing this requires a new mindset. We need to record our blessings in our gratitude journal, and this will help us never forget. It is such a simple thing to do, yet so empowering in helping us remember the goodness and mercy of God in our everyday lives. This is why the

Lord required daily performances during the Law of Moses, so the people would stay on the true course that always pointed them to Christ and His Atonement. Practicing gratitude daily in our prayers, our thoughts and actions, and our journals will help us live in thanksgiving at all times because we will never forget our blessings in prosperity or poverty.

Journaling Moment of Joy

Just as the records of God's dealings with His people helped them stay on the strait and narrow path, so will your gratitude journal help you and your descendants stay true to the faith. Record in your gratitude journal something that will be a reminder in all things to live in thanksgiving daily.

How Do We Create an Awareness, Which in Turn Fosters a Feeling of Gratitude?

When we have a vision of our purpose in life, appreciate those around us, and recognize the plethora of blessings we enjoy, we can begin to foster and possess a grateful heart. Strive for an "attitude of gratitude"—to feel a sense of appreciation for anything you have. We need eyes to see, ears to hear, and a heart to feel these sensations. Feel appreciation for your blessings from above and the personal kindnesses shown to you on a daily basis. Think to thank! Loving-kindness is the balm of Gilead; it always brings joy to the receiver and the giver. Seek to create within your mind and heart a disposition to always express thanksgiving in simple and sensitive ways.

While serving in the temple, I learned many simple and profound truths that temple workers easily practice. Because they know their purpose in the Lord's house, they seek to serve with loving-kindness. They seek to help the patrons who come to worship and serve in the Lord's holy house. They are inspired with compassion and expressions of love. They lead with love. They seek to serve. Their joy is in helping and doing good. This is what people do when they are in the Lord's house. They have purpose. They appreciate those around them. They act upon good feelings and joy in serving others. The fastest, simplest way to foster the awareness necessary to practice gratitude is by turning outward, looking beyond ourselves, and finding purpose in serving others.

Journaling Moment of Joy

Make a list of some people who need love, and then express gratitude for them with a simple gift, note, or compliment.

How Does Our Heart Become a Grateful Heart?

When you want something badly enough, it will come to reside in your heart. Following the visit of our beloved Savior, the people in the Book of Mormon received the love of God in their hearts and in turn received a multitude of blessings, including happiness. As the scripture states, "Surely there could not be a happier people among all the people who had been created by the hand of God" (4 Nephi 1:16).

Prior to the Savior's coming to the Nephites, the people fasted and prayed and became firm in their faith and strong in their humility. They were made holy and sanctified because they yielded their hearts to God (see Helaman 3:35). It is having a desire for gratitude that provoked the prayer of poet George Herbert: "Thou that hast giv'n so much to me, give one thing more, a gratefull heart" (from "The Temple," 1633). We need God's help to have a grateful heart. I remember that when I realized this I felt like all I had to do was ask. But I was wrong. I had to work with the same devotion and effort I applied to all my prayers. I had to start my gratitude journal. I had to begin thinking constantly about remembering to be grateful. I needed to express gratitude. I needed to look at all things with an eye of gratitude. I needed to count my blessings. Slowly but surely, I began to see and feel gratitude all around me. It became something that not only enveloped me but that also wanted to burst forth from my soul. I couldn't say thank you enough. I began to live a new way—and gratitude was in everything I thought about and did. Please understand that as I speak of this, I realize how much more I need to be and acknowledge my own nothingness without the help of the Lord (see Mosiah 4:5, 11; Helaman 12:7; Alma 26:11–12). In everything we have and are, there is a gift from God the Holy Ghost provides (see Moroni 10:8–18) that leads to redemption and exaltation (see

2 Nephi 25:23). We were created unto good works through the grace of God (see Ephesians 2:10), and we should continually think with thanksgiving and gratitude upon the tender mercies of the Lord (see Moroni 10:3).

Cultivating a Grateful Heart and Expressing Gratitude

> *A grateful heart doesn't just happen; it becomes an intense and passionate labor of love.*

Gratitude, like any virtue, requires desire and effort on our part in order to be cultivated within us. I have found there are some key actions we can take that help nurture gratitude in our lives.

1. Find ways to remember the goodness and mercy of God

We need to follow Moroni's admonition: "Behold, I would exhort you that when ye shall read these things, if it be wisdom in God that ye should read them, that ye would remember how merciful the Lord hath been unto the children of men, from the creation of Adam even down until the time that ye shall receive these things, and ponder it in your hearts" (Moroni 10:3). There is no other way!

I wore a penny in my shoe to remember this and many other things I needed to do for many years. I gave out thousands of pennies over the years to the youth and their leaders at seminary morningsides and firesides all over the United States. I would take off my shoe and show them my penny. Then I would explain that when I felt it, I remembered to be grateful and to be a good boy. Remembering was easy because I could always feel the penny. Weeks later, after the morningside or fireside, I would meet some of the teenagers, and they would say, "I know you. You're the penny man." We would laugh and then talk about remembering to be grateful and good. How great was my joy when I walked in to give a talk to the Eugene Oregon Stake and one of the Institute teachers greeted me with a happy smile, pulled off his shoe, and produced the penny I had given him over seven years ago. Gratitude filled my soul. He remembered.

Pondering on the goodness of God is one of the most wonderful experiences of my life—and a gratitude journal is a great way to capture those moments. I started my first gratitude journal in 2004, and it was an empowering experience. The very essence of it was recording the goodness and mercy of God in my life. As I was recently rereading that journal, I noticed the constant and recurring fact that everything—and I mean everything—in life bears witness to the tender mercies of God.

I take the liberty of sharing my journal from many years ago. It is simple but meaningful to me and helped me stay on track.

May 4

I am thankful for all of these things:

I can see. I can hear. I can walk. I can even run. I am grateful for my body, with all its magnificent functions that work. I can read and write. I love to hear the sounds of beautiful music. I am continually amazed at the beauty of my wife's gorgeous garden. It makes me think of Heavenly Father when I see it.

I can breathe. I am thankful for all the medicines I take to keep me alive. I am grateful to my doctors. I'm thankful for my computer and all that it can do. My cup runneth over with gratitude, and I know where all of my blessings come from. I'm grateful for my Savior and His infinite and atoning sacrifice.

May 5

Grateful for all things! Preciousness of time makes me want to work hard. This morning Wilford Woodruff taught me, "There is no peace or enjoyment in life without serving God and His children" [paraphrased]. *I never cease to be amazed by the goodness and mercy of God in all things.*

If we look carefully, we will notice that the grace of God is in everything and is everywhere. As we notice these things, we will be filled with thanksgiving and gratitude. We will be drawn to our Savior and our Heavenly Father.

Journaling Moment of Joy

Stop. Close your eyes. Now open them with a grateful heart and record ten things you are grateful for. See? You are nurturing the seed of a grateful heart.

2. Create visual reminders

Gospel doctrines are like vitamins. They only last so long in our system and have to be replenished often. That's why the Lord didn't say to partake once a month or occasionally, when you feel like it. He said to feast upon the word of God because, as President Eyring says, our faith has a short shelf life, and we need easy ways to remind ourselves (see "Spiritual Preparedness: Start Early and Be Steady," *Ensign*, November 2005). Visual reminders are incredibly effective. Put signs up all over the house, in the car, on the mirror, and on a card in a wallet or purse to remind us to be grateful. Remembering is the key factor to retaining gratitude in our hearts. Turn some of the more common aspects of your life into reminders: remember to be thankful when the telephone rings, when the car starts, when you sit down to rest for a moment, or when you walk into the chapel. Any other thing you do on a regular basis can serve as a reminder to be grateful.

I have become very aware of the power of reminders. President Spencer W. Kimball said

"Remembrance is the seed of gratitude which is the seed of generosity. Gratitude for the remission of sins is the seed of charity, the pure love of Christ."

(Henry B. Eyring, "Remembrance and Gratitude," *Ensign*, November 1989)

that *remember* is the most important word in the English language. It is an important key to having gratitude in our hearts all of the time.

For example, as a practicing dentist, my mind would be riveted to the work, but I also needed to remember to show gratitude and love to everyone, so in my dental office in each operatory, I put a little sign just above the intercom. It was simply one word: *Remember.* I would see that sign every time I pushed the button. I would see that word every time I turned away from the chair. It became a constant reminder in my life of the goodness of God and the goodness of my patients, and it reminded me to be kind and loving to everyone as Jesus would do. Visual reminders can be an empowering blessing to help us do good and be full of gratitude. Today, as I sit typing in my office, I look above my computer to a large 8"x 24" sign with one word: *Remember.*

The Lord, in His goodness, is very aware of what mortals need to remember: the goodness of God, the infinite Atonement and suffering of our Savior, and the importance of keeping the commandments. He instituted the sacrament as a way to help us be grateful and remember. The very purpose of the burnt offerings and sacrifice from the time of Adam to the coming of Christ was to remember the sacrifice of the Lord and His infinite Atonement.

Journaling Moment of Joy

Ponder and meditate upon our Savior's Atonement. Think of your blessings. Think where you would be without the Atonement. Read 2 Nephi 9. The Spirit will touch your heart, and gratitude will fill your soul. Now record your feelings in your journal.

3. Make it a family affair, or get a gratitude companion

Living a life of gratitude is so much easier if we have someone to talk with about it. The more we talk about it, the more gratitude we reflect in our lives. Make it a regular part of family home evening and discussions around the dinner table. When we pray with a grateful heart, we will see that our children will learn to pray like us. Gratitude is contagious.

We should use self-talk to remind ourselves about gratitude. Talking about gratitude brings it to the forefront of our minds. What we think about is what we eventually do, so when we think about gratitude, we will find ourselves having a sense of gratitude. Our hearts will change, and we will have an overwhelming desire to go about doing good. Look to see the good. Seeing, feeling, and observing the good, especially when good is not obvious, empowers us to act and not be acted upon. We are thus in control of ourselves. Rather than looking for what went wrong, try to catch people doing good, any good. By catching others doing good and expressing gratitude to them for it, we not only reinforce the good being done, but we also open the way for greater happiness and joy in their lives and our own. Honest and genuine praise of others brings with it a sense of thanksgiving for the receiver and the giver. Both will be grateful for the experience.

Looking to see gratitude is a wonderful virtue. My sweetheart took me by the arm the other day and said, "Come with me." I was excited; I knew she would show me something wonderful, as she always does. As we walked into the bedroom and looked out the window, there was a panoramic view of the most beautiful flowering cherry tree I had ever seen. She looked at me tenderly and said, "Isn't that absolutely beautiful?" Her sense of gratitude has always drawn her to the beauty of the creation of earth. She notices the handiwork of God and draws strength from it. She has had wonderful, strengthening experiences with gratitude in her life.

Journaling Moment of Joy

We need to count our blessings. A daily ritual of gratitude, even for just a minute, can change our lives. Take a minute today. Pull out your gratitude journal, and for sixty seconds, write down everything good you can think of. Then notice how you feel.

4. Record our feelings of gratitude

I know this works, as I have done it for many years. Counting and recording our blessings will help us remember. Recording my own feelings of gratitude has become an eye-opening and empowering experience for me. These are some ideas I use to help me do this effectively:

- I record all the tender mercies of the Lord, which are neverending, and as I recall them, I am drawn to the Lord through gratitude.
- I record all the blessings I receive concerning our family. This has resulted in an overwhelming desire to love and serve my family.
- I record all the blessings of the magnificence of my body. For example, I can breathe. Our autonomic nervous system automatically creates the action. Miraculous! My heart beats sixty to eighty times a minute, all automatically. I could go on about each individual organ and all the processes of

> our body and the purity and power of it and how it works miraculously. My brain can recognize that all of these things are a gift from God. This creates a sense of indebtedness, which helps gratitude take root in my soul—a good way to start this recognition is with a gratitude journal.

We will be amazed at the results of looking for gratitude and recording our feelings in regards to being grateful. We will come to see that gratitude is the parent of all virtues.

Journaling Moment of Joy

Think of the organs and systems of your body and how they work together to keep you functioning. Now take away your most precious one, then another, then another. Stop. Now express your gratitude for each of those things. I have done this. It is empowering because you will be filled with gratitude and thanksgiving, not just to overflowing but also to everlasting joy for your blessings. We are living miracles by the hand of God. Don't forget to record your feelings.

5. Express our gratitude

Say it—Express gratitude on a regular basis to family, friends, and coworkers. Everyone will be blessed. When we show gratitude to others, their hearts are touched. "Thanks so much for . . . . You made my day." "Your e-mail just gave me a boost. You are so kind." "Sweetheart, thanks for washing the car." And the list goes on.

Write it—Write a thank-you note, an e-mail, or a text at least every month to someone who has blessed your life.

Pray it—Prayer is worship (see Alma 33:3). We praise God and express thanksgiving for all things. The essence of prayer is to express gratitude. President Gordon B. Hinckley admonished: Get on your knees and thank the Lord for his bounties. "Cultivate a spirit of thanksgiving for the blessing of life and for the marvelous gifts and privileges each of us enjoy. The Lord has said that the meek shall inherit the earth. (See Matt. 5:5.) I cannot escape the interpretation that meekness implies a spirit of gratitude as opposed to an attitude of self-sufficiency, an acknowledgment of a greater power beyond oneself, a recognition of God, and an acceptance of his commandments. This is the beginning of wisdom" (Gordon B. Hinckley, "With All Thy Getting Get Understanding," *Ensign*, August 1988).

President Ezra Taft Benson reminded us, "We need to be more grateful. I think there is no true character without gratitude. It is one of the marks of a real strong character to have a feeling of thanksgiving and gratitude for blessings. We need more of that spirit in our homes, in our daily associations, in the Church, everywhere. It doesn't cost anything, and it is so easy to cultivate" (*God, Family, Country* [Salt Lake City: Deseret Book Company, 1974], 202).

Gratitude Fuels Consecration

I learned from King Benjamin that gratitude often produces a feeling of indebtedness. He taught this principle during his great sermon at the temple: "And now, in the first place, he hath created you, and granted unto you your lives, for which ye are indebted unto him. And secondly, he doth require that ye should do as he hath commanded you; for which if ye do, he doth immediately bless you; and therefore he hath paid you. And ye are still indebted unto him, and are, and will be, forever and ever; therefore, of what have ye to boast?" (Mosiah 2:23–24).

And thus we are unprofitable servants (see Mosiah 2:21). With these facts firmly entrenched in our minds, it is all we can do to give everything we have in return.

Journaling Moment of Joy

Take just a moment to thank someone and express gratitude to him or her. Then, in a special, quiet place, thank Heavenly Father for all things great and small, troublesome and pleasurable, and you will see how "all things shall work together for your good, if ye walk uprightly and remember" (D&C 90:24). Record the experience in your gratitude journal.

The Lord has asked His people to consecrate their lives to the building up of the kingdom of God. When we so consecrate our lives, we dedicate and set apart our time, talents, and material goods. Consecration is closely related to the depth of our conversion to the Savior and the gratitude we possess in our souls. Through consecration, we truly sacrifice all things for the Lord. We begin the process of purification of our own lives, and in turn, we become better able to bless our brothers and sisters so they too can enjoy eternal life. Consecration is an attitude as well as an observable act of goodness.

Gratitude truly is empowering through the grace of God.

PART II:

Gratitude Is within Every Virtue

Chapter 4

GRATITUDE: THE PARENT OF ALL VIRTUES

Gratitude is either a beginning to, a result of, or an innate part of every virtue.

CICERO SAID, "GRATITUDE IS NOT only the greatest of virtues, but the parent of all the others." Cicero understood the empowering nature of gratitude. Can gratitude and love be the powerful engine that motivates our souls? I suggest it is! If we are thankless and fail to express gratitude and love, we will have little passion for life. Our faith will be weak. Hope will be dormant. Charity will be absent. Virtues without gratitude are incomplete.

Gratitude Is the Gateway to All Virtues

Gratitude is either a beginning to, a result of, or an innate part of every virtue. Remember the purpose of this book is to focus on the empowering nature of the virtue of gratitude that will lead us to a multiplicity of virtues and affect our lives for good. Ponder how a grateful heart can and will change your life forever. Ponder as well this wonderful paragraph by this beautiful and insightful sister: "Any plan, any course, that can let me think of him [our Savior] more often, help me to acknowledge his hand in everything around me, feel gratitude for every aspect of my life, and serve him more readily is an okay road to take. And he teaches me as we go. I'm finally seeing that what I thought was mundane and bothersome is really meaningful and beautiful. And you can, too" (Mary B. Kirk, "Finding Holiness in Everyday Life," in Dawn Hall Anderson, Susette Fletcher Green, and Dlora Hall Dalton, eds., *Clothed with Charity: Talks from the 1996 Women's Conference* [Salt Lake City, Utah: Deseret Book Company, 1997], 116).

This little exercise to feel gratitude for every aspect of our lives will demonstrate why gratitude affects everything to one degree or another. It is essential in acknowledging the Lord's hand in all things. Then, if we take the time to express gratitude in a journal for these blessings, we can lock them into our hearts. As we practice this, we will come to understand the power of expressing gratitude.

Gratitude for the goodness, loving-kindness, and tender mercies of Heavenly Father and our Savior is the beginning of being able to accept the laws of God. Gratitude creates a sense of indebtedness, which inspires us to be willing to receive and accept the laws of God. When we understand and appreciate each law and the blessings associated with that law, gratitude will empower us to go forward, not just with accepting but also with embracing the law and putting it into practice. We will even be grateful for the law of opposition, so we will act positively when faced with trials and adversity. We need to accept and embrace the law of opposition in all things (see 2 Nephi 2:11) and know that if we experience great adversity, it will be for our good (see D&C 122:5–9).

President Hinckley has taught us the attitude to have when facing opposition: "All of us have problems. We face them every day. How grateful I am that we have difficult things to wrestle with. They keep us young, if that is possible. They keep us alive. They keep us going. They keep us humble. They pull us down to our knees to ask the God of heaven for help in solving them. Be grateful for your problems, and know that somehow there will come a solution. . . . Just do the best you can, but be sure it is your very best. Then leave it in the hands of the Lord" ("A Challenging Time—A Wonderful Time," An Evening with President Gordon B. Hinckley, CES Fireside, 7 February 2003).

With gratitude for all things great and small, we recognize and accept adversity and blessings in our lives. With a grateful heart, we can accept and embrace life's experiences as they come. We are filled with gratitude when we overcome or endure our trials and tribulations.

I vividly remember being introduced to the power of pain. Ankylosing Spondylitis is a painful back condition associated with spinal arthritis, and I have dealt with it since I was twenty years old. Then, in my midseventies, I had an unknown collection of spinal fluid pressing on my spinal cord to exacerbate the pain. When the intense shocks of pain would radiate through my back, I would wonder how I could stand it and when it would ever end. But it was then that gratitude came to the rescue. I realized how grateful I was when I didn't have pain. Pain became my teacher. Pain taught me what a blessing it was when I was free from it, something I had previously completely taken for granted. Consequently, this gratitude helped me get through my future bouts of pain.

It really all comes down to the attitude with which we address a situation. Two people can be faced with the same situation, and one can become hardhearted, angry, and resentful, while the other can be full of gratitude and humility, being drawn to the Lord. This is exemplified as we read, "But behold, because of the exceedingly great length of the war between the Nephites and the Lamanites many had become hardened, because of the exceedingly great length of the war; and many were softened because of their afflictions, insomuch that they did humble themselves before God, even in the depth of humility" (Alma 62:41).

Another way of thinking of this is captured in this quote: "Boiling water hardens eggs but softens carrots . . . so a long drawn-out war causes some to be hardened, while others are softened in their afflictions. Each of us must decide how anything outside will affect us, negatively or positively" (D. Kelly Ogden and Andrew C. Skinner, *Verse by Verse: The Book of Mormon, Vol. Two, Alma 30 through Moroni* [Salt Lake City: Deseret Book Company, 2011], 78).

These differing attitudes are also displayed in the way people address their wealth, as in the Book of Mormon:

> And the people of Nephi began to prosper again in the land, and began to multiply and to wax exceedingly strong again in the land. And they began to grow exceedingly rich. But notwithstanding

> their riches, or their strength, or their prosperity, they were not lifted up in the pride of their eyes; neither were they slow to remember the Lord their God; but they did humble themselves exceedingly before him. Yea, they did remember how great things the Lord had done for them, that he had delivered them from death, and from bonds, and from prisons, and from all manner of afflictions, and he had delivered them out of the hands of their enemies. And they did pray unto the Lord their God continually, insomuch that the Lord did bless them, according to his word, so that they did wax strong and prosper in the land. (Alma 62:48–51)

These two examples demonstrate how having an attitude of gratitude will determine how we respond in every situation, both for good and for bad. The gratitude we possess becomes the barometer of our behavior.

Journaling Moment of Joy

Take a moment to record your feelings in your gratitude journal concerning the blessings of the laws of God.

Chapter 5
EXAMPLES OF GRATITUDE

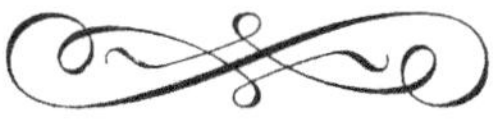

Gratitude can become our way of life.

An Attitude of Gratitude

Having an attitude of gratitude can help us look for positive aspects in our lives in the midst of adversity. A story a friend told me many years ago proves the point that a good attitude can make the difference in everybody's life. It was picture day at school, and the little girl talking with her mother said, "Oh, Mom, what dress can I wear?" Her mother said, "Sweetheart, let's have you wear that beautiful new white dress." She was so excited. That morning, she was very first at the bus stop. She drew a little line in the dirt on the side of the road and stood there straight and true. She thought, *Picture day at school, and I'm first in line for the bus.*

Along came a car she didn't notice. Turning slightly, the car hit a chuckhole, and mud splattered all over her. She was a mess. She began to cry and ran home to her little house just a block away. "Mommy, Mommy, look, look. I'm ruined. My dress is ruined." Her mother said, "Sweetheart, you left so early, there is still time. Quick, let's put on another dress." They put on her second-best dress, and she ran back to the bus stop. Just as she got there, the bus was almost ready to pull away. She reached for the door, but the bus driver didn't see her and slammed the door right on her nose. Blood went everywhere. The bus driver said, "Oh dear, I'm sorry, little sweetheart." She helped her in and gave her a hankie, but there she was, with a nosebleed right on the bus. Tears streaming down her cheeks, she rode to school.

When she got there, her nose had stopped bleeding, and things seemed to be okay, but during first recess, her day got even worse. Some of the boys were having their typical snowball fights, and one snowball went the wrong direction and hit her right in the eye. Oh, it was icy, and it hurt. Her eye began to swell, and tears streamed out of her good eye.

Lunchtime recess brought another challenge. Gleaming in the distance on the playground were her favorite—the trick bars. She climbed to the top and waved to a friend, then lost her balance and fell. She landed on her arm and heard a snap. She yelled out in pain, but as she did so, she noticed something shiny on the ground, and she clutched it in her one good hand. She ran as best she could to the teacher, who took her quickly to the school nurse. The nurse said, "I'm afraid you have to go to the doctor. Your arm may be broken." They put the arm in a sling and called her mother.

The girl went outside to wait. There she stood—scabby nose, eye swollen shut, arm in a sling, and wearing her second-best dress. A smile came to her face. Her mother pulled up and, while helping her into the car, said, "How can you smile at a time like this?" The girl replied, "Oh, Mommy, Mommy, it's my lucky day! I found a quarter."

The point of this sweet little story is that this little girl overlooked her difficulty and focused on something that brought her joy. We can choose to have an attitude of gratitude, and it only takes training our minds to do it. In the midst of tribulation and adversity, there are moments as shiny as a quarter on a playground. It is in looking for the good that we can overcome the devastation of adversity. Difficult? Yes. Doable? Of course . . . in the strength of the Lord.

When gratitude becomes part of us, we feel the grace of God that enables us to go forward in the strength of the Lord.

Gratitude gives rise to compassion and empathy. In simple terms, we care for others when we are thankful. Here is another story to illustrate.

It was almost Christmas, and the long list of to-dos that had to get done before the holiday was worrying me. I was grateful for my family, but I was overloaded with myriad pressing items.

Everywhere I turned, there were things that needed my attention. After work, I hurried to the store that would close in just a half hour. Outside the department store, I noticed a man with no legs, resting on a little rolling pad, selling pencils. The man looked cold, and no one was stopping to buy. As I hurried past him into the store, I thought, *How sad. I should help, but I just haven't the time. So much to get done! Maybe later.* I did my shopping and was one of the last people out of the store when my mind returned to the little man. He was gone. My heart sank, and I was pricked by guilt. I had so many blessings. What was I thinking? Was I really too busy to reach out and help another? With a heavy heart, I got in my car and headed home. It was late and time for bed. Sleep wouldn't come. I had compassion and empathy for this child of God who was doing his best with the little he had. He wasn't begging. He was selling his wares. I got out of bed and knelt, pleading, "Please give me another chance, Heavenly Father."

As soon as work ended the next day, I thought again of the little man who was trying his best. I wanted to make amends. As I ran toward the store, I could see him sitting on his small, tattered pad. I knelt beside him, whispered words of encouragement, and thanked him for helping me remember all of my blessings. I bought some pencils and stuffed a large bill into the man's hat, then I hugged him, and we both smiled. I walked slowly to my car, filled with love as I thanked my Heavenly Father for this precious tender mercy in my life. Suddenly the list of things I needed to do didn't seem nearly as important. In that moment, I felt the peace that invariably comes when we act on our concern for God's children. Life was good. Gratitude filled my heart, and I had hope within my soul.

Gratitude Motivates Many Virtues

Gratitude enhances our concern for others and causes us to reach out to others in friendliness. We become approachable, outgoing, pleasant, and sociable. We recognize that everyone needs friends, and everyone needs attention and love. Gratitude enhances our capacity to have better personal relationships.

Gratitude for *having* gives us the desire to experience gratitude for *giving*. When a person has gratitude, enough is enough. Having gratitude makes having possessions unnecessary because you are grateful for whatever you have. You are then released from "keeping up with the Joneses." With gratitude firmly entrenched in your soul, the capacity to give is your expression of gratitude to others. The Savior Himself taught that it is better to give than to receive (see Acts 20:35). This generosity is born of a grateful heart. When receiving a gift, our thoughts turn to expressing gratitude to all; our gratitude is not limited to just the giver of the gift. The Lord encourages generosity (see Matthew 10:8; Luke 3:11; 6:35, 38; Acts 3:6; 2 Corinthians 9:7; Jacob 2:17; Alma 34:29; D&C 56:16). I have had the blessing of being on the receiving end of some wonderful generosity. I had the privilege of working with a group of men, one of whom had been very kind and generous to me. I gave him a book I had written, and he was so full of gratitude that he wanted all to receive this same book. He quietly gave me a check and asked me to please give a copy to everyone. Now, this certainly wasn't my agenda when I gave him the book! I was surprised

> *"Our prayers for others flow more easily than those for ourselves. This shows we are made to live by charity."*
>
> (C.S. Lewis)

and thrilled by his actions, but truly, he was more blessed than I was in that moment. His gratitude was overwhelming, and he sought to bring joy to all. (Thanks, KC.) Gratitude is spontaneous, contagious, and exponential in its growth.

Gratitude Inspires Us to Action

The Lord wants us to be grateful. This is why we are to ponder the goodness and mercy of God (see Moroni 10:3). Gratitude is so empowering that it ignites us to action. This is why Alma asked those questions of conscience in making the mighty change. When you feel gratitude deeply, your life will be changed forever.

This great truth was demonstrated in a tender moment while I was presiding at the Provo MTC. A young missionary was struggling in every way possible. He was frustrated, overwhelmed, and very anxious to go home. It was evident that he was not ready or prepared to serve as a missionary. The branch president explained that the young man was upset at everybody, his companion was distraught, the district was upset, and everyone was concerned about the young missionary's behavior. I invited him in. He expressed distaste for the mission and the Missionary Training Center and explained why he really didn't want to come on a mission in the first place. We visited at length, and I hoped the whole time that I could assess his needs and real concerns. He continually expressed his desire to go home and get out of this trying and troubling situation. Since we had several hours before he would be able to leave, simply because of packing and transportation concerns, I suggested that we continue to visit. I asked him questions like, "How do you feel about your Heavenly Father?" Indeed, he loved his Heavenly Father. "How do you feel about life?" Then he expressed that he was distraught, discouraged, and overwhelmed. He didn't like life. He didn't understand life. He was beside himself.

Then the Spirit taught me what to teach: teach of Christ; preach of Christ—all things of Christ. I was to teach of the magnificent and eternal atoning sacrifice and how it can heal us through its enabling power, for it is through Christ that we are nurtured and blessed in our weaknesses. We talked at great length about the Lord Jesus Christ and His Atonement. Then the missionary's heart began to soften, his mind began to understand, his heart began to feel overwhelming gratitude for his beloved Savior Jesus Christ and all He had done for him. His eyes lightened. His countenance changed. The Holy Spirit had enlightened him. And after this tender moment, I again asked, "How do you feel?" And with tears streaming down his face, he said, "Oh, President Pinegar, I want to serve a mission. I love my Heavenly Father and my Savior. I am so grateful. I need help. I understand better the goodness and mercy of my Heavenly Father and my Savior in my life. I was just mixed up and wanted to get out of here, but not anymore. I want to do it. I want to be a missionary."

He had received a blessing. His heart was broken, and his spirit was contrite. He understood.

He was full of appreciation and gratitude. He stayed and served his mission. He understood and appreciated the Atonement and its power to heal. He had a mighty change as he was empowered by the Atonement and the power of the Holy Ghost. My heart swelled with eternal joy for the tender mercies of God our Father and our beloved Savior, Jesus Christ. And life was good because this young missionary felt the love of God as he came to understand and appreciate the infinite and eternal Atonement of Christ.

Gratitude to Breathe—A Defining Moment

It is interesting to note that after we have a life-threatening experience, we are anxious to reconsecrate our lives to the service of our God and our fellowmen because we are full of gratitude for life itself. When we are about to lose it all, we are willing to promise everything because the blessings in those moments mean everything to us. We always have gratitude in our hearts; sometimes it just needs to be awakened and expressed.

Thinking of threatening experiences reminds me of a scary yet magnificent reconsecrating moment in my life. It brought gratitude for my blessings and became a growing experience for me. We were sitting at the dinner table, and my sweetheart had made the most delicious tacos. I was eating them, and unbeknownst to me, I had a little malady where my esophageal sphincter, the valve that lets the food into the stomach, wasn't working—it was closed. My food began to fill my esophagus all the way up to my epiglottis. But I didn't know that was happening, so I decided it was time for a drink of milk. As I swallowed the milk, it covered my epiglottis, and I could not breathe. I looked around at my family, but however I tried, I couldn't make a sound. My sweetheart asked, "What's wrong? Honey, what can I do?" This went on for many more seconds, which, in my panic, felt much longer, and my children cried, "Daddy, Daddy, what can we do?"

I struggled to breathe but to no avail. Five more seconds went by, my mind flashed, and I thought my life was over. I thought, *Heavenly Father, I've been a good boy. I've been trying to do what's right. I don't want to die. What should I do*? Finally, I was inspired to trigger my gag reflex, which dislodged the food. I took a breath! To be without air is to be without life. That huge gulp of oxygen brought instant gratitude. Now, every time I take a deep, deep breath, I remember that one breath of air when I thought my life was about to end. I want you to know I still appreciate the capacity to swallow and to breathe, and I am grateful for the tender mercies of God. Appreciation is indeed the precursor to gratitude. Life is fragile, and we are all a heartbeat away from the other side. It is so important to make it our quest to consecrate all we have to the Lord before it is too late.

Gratitude to God produces perseverance, dedication, devotion, diligence, and good works, which are all part of consecration. Having an eye single to the glory of God is born of gratitude. The blessing of being diligent is always rewarded with increased thanksgiving toward Heavenly Father and our Savior. Diligence is more than work because it entails a caring attitude and a single-mindedness of doing our best. Think about it—when you are diligent in keeping the commandments, don't you feel gratitude and love for Heavenly Father and our Savior? Pondering with gratitude in our hearts will keep us consecrated to the things of God.

Gratitude through Perseverance

When we are grateful for the word of God, we feast upon it and hold fast to it because it leads us to Christ and empowers us to do good. This virtue will cause us to live by every word which proceedeth forth from the mouth of God (see D&C 84:43–46). This virtue helps us hold to the iron rod, which leads us to the tree of life and to partaking of the love of God. The word of God is our Liahona for life (see Alma 37:38–44). It will tell us all things that we should do (see 2 Nephi 32:3). The preaching of the word leads us to do justly and has the greatest power upon our minds (see Alma 31:5).

I remember my family's experience with studying the scriptures together. I had come to understand the importance and value of scripture study for our family. My sweetheart and I were committed to having scripture time, and we persevered. On Sundays, I'd go into my room for a couple of hours and research a topic, and then that afternoon, I'd call the children around and we'd study about faith, charity, prayer, any doctrine that seemed important at the time concerning the gospel of Jesus Christ. Then, every morning, we'd get up and read a few scriptures about that topic and attempt to apply them to our lives. That experience later became my first book, *You, Your Family, and the Scriptures.*

Over the years, our scripture study continued. When our daughter Kelly was ready to go on her mission, I was surprised when she stood at the pulpit, turned to look at me, and said, "Do you know what it's like to be raised by a man like this? I learned to detest his little squeaky voice when I was only seven years old as he called through the door, 'Scripture time, Kelly,' and we would all get up and begin to study the scriptures." Then her voice quavered, and tears filled her eyes. She continued. "Oh, how I thank my God now, for that's when I learned to love the word of God."

Gratitude to God for Our Bodies Is Reflected in Dressing Modestly

We express gratitude for our bodies in modest clothing. Noelle Pikus-Pace is an Olympic skeleton racer who won the silver medal in the 2014 Olympic Games. Throughout her time in

Sochi, everyone could always see her wearing her Young Women medallion around her neck. She was a great role model for women and young women around the world.

Noelle shared a wonderful story about modesty in her new book *Focused.* Before her first Olympic appearance, she was invited to a national media summit. She was supposed to bring a variety of outfits for the photo shoot, including athletic wear and Sunday best. Noelle was rushed from one interview to the next, culminating in a photo shoot involving many outfit changes in just a few minutes' time in a makeshift dressing room. For her last photo, she was handed a beautiful red dress she hadn't brought in her clothing selection. All of the female athletes, she was told, were wearing red dresses to support healthy hearts. The dress she was given had spaghetti straps and was very short. How could she wear it?

Worried to be the only athlete who didn't cooperate, she hesitated. But only for a moment. "When it came down to it," she explained, "wearing the dress or not was a very easy decision for me to make, because I had already chosen to stand as a witness of God 'at all times and in all things, and in all places'" (Mosiah 18:9). She handed the dress back and said, "I want to be modest. It's just who I am, and I am very sorry, but I can't wear this." Expecting the handler to be frustrated, Noelle was surprised when the woman told her Noelle was a good Christian girl and she respected her beliefs. She found something else for her to wear, and though the replacement dress wasn't nearly as cute or flattering, it was modest.

Four years later, when Noelle attended the same media summit for the Sochi Olympics, the same handler was there to help her. As Noelle entered the room, she gave her a hug and said, "I remember you! You're that good Christian girl. We don't have any immodest clothing for you to wear this time." Noelle smiled and was so grateful she had made the choice to stand up for her beliefs. Her choice to be modest left a positive impression on not only the woman helping her but on thousands of women and girls watching her around the world (Excerpt from *Focused* by Noelle Pikus-Pace, quoted in "Olympian Faced with Modesty Dilemma at Photo Shoot," ldsliving.com).

Grateful for Repentance and Forgiveness

> *"Remembrance is the seed of gratitude which is the seed of generosity. Gratitude for the remission of sins is the seed of charity, the pure love of Christ."*
>
> (Henry B. Eyring, "Remembrance and Gratitude," *Ensign*, November 1989)

Repentance is an expression of gratitude for the infinite Atonement. Gratitude helps us recognize and confess our sins. We express it with a broken heart and contrite spirit. It creates within us abhorrence for sin, the power to forsake sin, and a desire to make restitution for sin and forgive others. Gratitude fosters within us a desire to do good and is incredibly powerful when our hearts yield to those magnificent feelings that cause change. Indeed, gratitude is a catalyst of change. In other words, we repent.

I remember the day I took a test in my organic chemistry class my junior year at BYU. Chemistry was my major, and I was doing well in school. I was finishing the midterm exam, and I was struggling on one question. As I tried to think of the solution, I casually looked around and saw that the catalyst for the reaction that my neighbor had suggested was Ca++ with heat, as expressed by the delta sign, so I put it down too. It was one part of one answer on one test . . . half of 1 percent or less of the test grade. Could it matter? *Yes*! I was dishonest, and I would suffer for my sin. Little did I realize my neighbor had been observing many things on my paper, and the student on his left was likewise helping himself to my neighbor's answers. Four of us in a row had the same incorrect answer, so our teacher, Dr. Blackham, called us in to find out why we would all have such a weird answer.

The dilemma for me was that I was Dr. Blackham's home teacher too. He had interviewed the other students, and I was the last one. I knew I had been tempted and had cheated. Of course I could have rationalized and said I was 99.5 percent honest on the test, but that would not have changed the fact that I had cheated. His remarks began, "Ed, I am so sorry for bringing you in to talk about this one question. You didn't cheat, did you?" At that moment, I was tempted again. I didn't want to let him down, and I succumbed again to temptation and became a liar too.

Life went on, and ten years later, I was called to serve as a bishop at BYU. My first talk was on the honor code. That sin came to my mind, and wouldn't leave. I knew I had to seek forgiveness. Getting up all the courage I could muster, I called Dr. Blackham. I begged his forgiveness, and he was full of charity, even as our Savior would have been, and frankly forgave me and proceeded to tell me what a good man I had turned into. Relief came quickly. Joy filled my heart. The pain was gone, as was the guilt.

If we succumb to temptation, there is only one road back, and that is repentance and change—moving forward and praying for the strength to never yield to that temptation again. We can see that temptation is at every turn in our lives. It, like opposition, is always at work so we can choose, and when we choose wrongfully, repentance brings gratitude to Heavenly Father and our Savior and peace to the soul.

Journaling Moment of Joy

Remember to record in your gratitude journal the virtues connected to gratitude. Make it a special section, and you will be surprised at how each virtue will empower you to find a state of increased happiness and joy.

Gratitude becomes a key to righteousness.

Gratitude is the catalyst of change.

Gratitude is a cardinal empowering virtue in our lives.

Gratitude is an expression of our hearts, and the Lord "looketh on the heart" (1 Samuel 16:7) to discover our true level of gratefulness. We cannot fake our gratitude; in other words, there must be a genuine integrity behind our thankfulness, for the Lord loves those who have integrity in their hearts (see D&C 124:15, 20).

A gracious person is then the kind of person we will become, "for as he thinketh in his heart, so is he" (Proverbs 23:7). Those with pure hearts will be able to see God (see Matthew 5:8).

When we finally stand before the judgment bar of the Lord, part of our judgment is determined by our hearts. "For I, the Lord, will judge all men according to their works, according to the desire of their hearts" (D&C 137:9). We feel gratitude in our hearts, and we act upon that feeling, choosing to do good. The motivator of that choice is a grateful heart, the precursor to love, the great commandment. George Herbert, in his poem "Gratefulness," again reminds us, "Thou that hast given so much to me, give one thing more, a grateful heart. . . . Not thankful when it pleaseth me, as if Thy blessings had spare days, but such a heart, whose pulse may be Thy praise."

The desires of our hearts will determine our eternal blessings. Let us all seek to have a grateful heart.

PART III:
Living with a Grateful Heart

Chapter 6

GRATITUDE: THE KEY TO HAPPINESS

GRATITUDE IS THE MIRACULOUS, MAGNIFICENT, and marvelous key to the love of God, which is "desirable to make one happy" (1 Nephi 8:10). Gratitude should be rooted in our very hearts. We need faith, diligence, and patience to nurture its seed. Within the hearts of mankind, the Lord has planted many such seeds of His divine nature and character, which need to be nurtured—humility, love, faith, hope, charity, and many more. We need all of these characteristics, combined with gratitude in our hearts, to change and become like Christ, even as He is (see 3 Nephi 27:27).

A few years ago, when I was serving in the Manti Utah Temple, we were having our annual temple devotional. President Uchtdorf and his sweetheart Harriet were the speakers. It was a glorious day. Everyone felt a fulness of the Holy Spirit, and all were uplifted and edified. Following the meeting, we had a light lunch with our invited guests and President and Sister Uchtdorf. At the conclusion of our luncheon, President Uchtdorf gave a short expression of gratitude and then asked if anyone had a question he could answer. Several people asked questions, and the answers were well received. Then he asked for one last question. One of the sisters who had helped prepare the luncheon asked, "President Uchtdorf, what is it that we need to have in order to grow, to become, to be able to handle the burdens, problems, and trials we have in this life?" As I sat right across from him and looked into his eyes, I could see enlightenment. After a couple of seconds, he said, "Gratitude." My heart resonated with his response, knowing by spiritual witness that truth had been spoken. It is by the power of the Holy Ghost that we know the truth of all things (see Moroni 10:5).

Gratitude gives us new vision.

Gratitude gives us new vision and acts as a powerful shield. If we were nurtured with gratitude, we would experience no bitterness or resentment. There would be no wishing we were someone else. We would simply feel wonderful feelings, even euphoria. When we practice gratitude and live with a grateful heart, it's hard to believe the power that gratitude can manifest in our lives. From the empirical study found in chapter two, we can see that gratitude works from understanding both past blessings and present blessings, and therefore, we are better able to handle the pressure of the future. We must have gratitude for the past as well for the "now." It brings us closer to our Heavenly Father and our Savior.

Gratitude expressed can overcome desires to consume and possess. Sometimes people feel that having things is equal to being someone. But gratitude for the simple things of life soothes the mind from the obsession of possessions, fills the heart with joy, and infuses the mind with well-being. Gratitude destroys materialism.

Gratitude has the capacity to release us from greed and envy. Gratitude keeps our heart soft and broken and our spirit contrite. Gratitude helps us receive love and give love; it brings thanksgiving for all things and makes what matters most the most important, for gratitude understands.

Gratitude is an emotion. Emotions are often mercurial in one's life. The cerebral cortex is the part of the brain that makes rational decisions regardless of our emotions. We often need cortical override—logic over emotion—to behave in a moral and civil manner. We must be careful not to be subject to our negative emotional feelings during those times when we don't care about life. To make gratitude a power, we must make it part of our character. The saying by George D. Boardman, "Sow an act, and you reap a habit; sow a habit, and you reap a character; sow a character, and you reap a destiny," is surely true (*Phinneys' Calendar*, 1878, edited by Andrew Beers). *Gratitude can become a constant source of strength to others and ourselves.* Gratitude has no place for a self-defeating attitude. Gratitude has no place for being a pessimist about our life's lack of perfection. Gratitude helps us not only endure unbearable situations but also gain appreciation from the experience. We can uplift and nourish others. The next time we are in line waiting at the post office and patience seems to be wanting in everyone's demeanor, strike up a conversation. For example, you could note how amazing it is that we don't have to wait for the Pony Express to send our letters or that we don't have to carry them ourselves. We simply stand in line for ten minutes, and then the marvelous U.S. mail sends it all over the world. Patience is a virtue of gratitude. When we are grateful, we will be patient. When we have to wait for our doctors, we can be grateful that they can see us. Gratitude is so much more enjoyable than anger and resentment. We can build relationships born of genuine appreciation, gratitude, and praise with others.

Journaling Moment of Joy

Record your feelings about the empowering nature of gratitude and your pursuit to have a grateful heart.

Nurturing Gratitude in Others and in Our Own Hearts

Nurturing others—and ourselves, for that matter—in any principle or virtue requires a great deal of patience and love. It takes time to grasp and internalize this wonderful virtue, and we must be diligent and faithful in our efforts. We each need to discover gratitude for ourselves, literally becoming grateful individuals with a natural ability to feel and show that gratitude.

At Thanksgiving dinner, we have a tradition of going around the table and expressing gratitude for blessings in our lives. This is a good yearly family tradition that would be a great daily tradition. Expressing gratitude on a daily basis would be wonderful at dinnertime or bedtime, whether to a friend, a parent, a family member, or Heavenly Father in our prayers. It is a wonderful habit, and the result is a more satisfying, hopeful, and enjoyable life.

For whom should we be grateful? Everyone. We are a picture puzzle of life that includes associations with and learning experiences from teachers, family, friends, and acquaintances. We should be aware of all the people who have contributed to our lives, especially our mothers. Mothers truly are the ultimate nurturers.

In every leadership or relationship role, we are both teachers and learners. In life, teachers probably have the greatest influence on all humankind. All of us have felt gratitude at one time or another for those who have influenced us. The question is do we take the time to express thanksgiving to our teachers? This may be one of the great shortcomings of society. One thing we ought to commit to do is thank our teachers. We are the fruit of their labors. We become an extension of them, and we owe who we are, in part, to them.

A friend of mine recently found out that her favorite college dance teacher, whom she hadn't seen in over twenty years, had retired due to early-onset Alzheimer's. She didn't know if the teacher would even remember who she was, but she decided to take a few minutes to write her a card to thank her for the impact she'd had in her life. Later, she learned that the teacher's husband had quietly cried as he'd watched his wife's reaction to this small token of gratitude and that it had meant the world to this teacher to hear from one of her past students.

Stories like this are very tender to me. The students and missionaries I have had the honor of teaching are so incredibly kind. Whenever anyone expresses gratitude to me, I feel an increased desire to be better in every way. My heart overflows with gratitude for the opportunity to be a part of their lives. Gratitude truly changes hearts.

Gratitude for the past is essential in order to live in gratitude in the present. The growth of society and the development of civilization have given us amenities in life that no other generation has experienced. We are the blessed recipients of all those who have gone before, and we are indebted to all of our ancestors and those who have made these wonderful contributions to society. We need to show our gratitude for the past by leaving a legacy for those who follow. We need to plant a tree bearing the fruit of gratitude for all who come after us—a tree that can help feed the hearts of humankind. Then all might have a grateful heart.

Take a moment. Make a phone call, send an e-mail, text a message, write a note, but tell someone thank you. You will feel great, and you will make their day! "Gracias," "Danke," "Thank you"—however you say it, this verbal expression carries appreciation. Thank-you

Gratitude for tomorrow is wonderful as long as we live in gratitude today.

letters and special gifts act as symbols of gratitude. When people read them or see them, a flood of happy memories fills their hearts. Oh, the power of the expression of gratitude! When one is praised or thanked, it seems to perpetuate goodness in both the receiver and the giver, and the chain of gratitude goes on.

Journaling Moment of Joy

Record your feelings about the power of expressing thanks.

President Joseph F. Smith has taught:

> We are almost daily put under obligations to one another, especially to friends and acquaintances, and the sense of obligation creates within us feelings of thankfulness and appreciation

which we call gratitude. The spirit of gratitude is always pleasant and satisfying because it carries with it a sense of helpfulness to others; it begets love and friendship, and engenders divine influence. Gratitude is said to be the memory of the heart.

And where there is an absence of gratitude, either to God or man, there is the presence of vanity and the spirit of self-sufficiency. . . .

Naturally people feel grateful to those who have done them a kindness, and the feeling of gratitude is generally a sufficient compensation for those who have done a kind and unselfish act. But when one does a favor for another, and behind that favor is the secret and selfish intent that the gratitude awakened by the favor shall become a debt the receiver at some time and in some way must repay, then gratitude becomes a debt, an extortion, not a virtue.

An act of apparent kindness can never result in good when it is intended to put any man under obligations that deprive him of his freedom to act. That is the characteristic of a politician. It is buying up one's freedom, and such a bargain is worse upon the man who seeks to make it than Shylock's contract for a pound of flesh. (*Gospel Doctrine: Selections from the Sermons and Writings of Joseph F. Smith* [Salt Lake City: Deseret Book Company, 1939], 262.) ("Shylock's contract for a pound of flesh" is a reference to Shakespeare's *The Merchant of Venice*. Shylock was a Jewish moneylender who despised Christians. He had lost his own flesh, his daughter, to a Christian, and because of this, he was angry and sought revenge at all costs. To a merchant who had defaulted on a loan, Shylock tried to legally require of him a pound of his flesh, which would have killed the merchant.)

Gratitude is a forerunner to transformational growth as we begin to experience the "mighty change of heart" spoken of in the scriptures (see Mosiah 5:2–3; Alma 5:14). This mighty change has many steps and events within it, yet it is a continuum throughout life. Becoming perfected in Christ is a process. It also makes us teachable. President Henry B. Eyring taught: "To feel gratitude is to feel dependent. To recognize our dependence is what we mean by true humility. And humility is the absence of pride, the great enemy of learning. So the very generosity which is evident everywhere at this university creates for those with eyes to see and hearts to feel a sense of gratitude which in turn can make us better learners. That feeling of gratitude, if you nurture it carefully, will keep you teachable over a lifetime" ("Graduates Told to Be Lifelong Learners," *LDS Church News*, 28 June 1997).

We begin to make the mighty change as we are humble and easily entreated; thus we can come to the knowledge of the truth (Alma 23:5–6). This knowledge comes only through humility (see Alma 7:23, 13:28). With knowledge comes understanding. Understanding gives life to appreciation. Appreciation unleashes a grateful heart, and this gratitude becomes the catalyst to positive change. It has the power to help us do good. It is the key to a joyous and fulfilling life. Gratitude overcomes many negatives in life—just as faith overcomes doubt and fear, so likewise does gratitude overcome anger, adversity, hopelessness, and myriad other challenges we face in life. Gratitude truly is the positive pressure that pushes us forward with hope and all the joys of life even in our darkest hours. When our hearts are full of gratitude for the goodness of God, the love of God can enter our very beings, for we have changed for the better.

King Benjamin teaches us an eternal truth that inspires gratitude to God for all things:

> I say unto you, my brethren, that if you should render all the thanks and praise which your whole soul has power to possess, to that God who has created you, and has kept and preserved you, and has caused that ye should rejoice, and has granted that ye should live in peace one with another—
>
> I say unto you that if ye should serve him who has created you from

> the beginning, and is preserving you from day to day, by lending you breath, that ye may live and move and do according to your own will, and even supporting you from one moment to another—I say, if ye should serve him with all your whole souls yet ye would be unprofitable servants.
>
> And behold, all that he requires of you is to keep his commandments; and he has promised you that if ye would keep his commandments ye should prosper in the land; and he never doth vary from that which he hath said; therefore, *if ye do keep his commandments he doth bless you and prosper you.* (Mosiah 2:20–22, emphasis added)

If we were to read and reread King Benjamin's address on a regular basis, we would make a quantum leap in gaining gratitude. Gratitude is to life what the sun is to the vitality and energy of all growth. Gratitude edifies and lifts the soul, gives buoyancy to our spirit, and nurtures our relationships. It is the fundamental spiritual attitude that adds kindness and warmth to our lives. Where gratitude is present, envy withdraws in shame and selfishness flees in humiliation. A plethora of virtues unfold, bringing peace, love, and serenity—these are the harvest of a life filled with gratitude. God planted within us the precious seeds of gratitude; let us cultivate this gift with care and thanksgiving, for upon it depends all lasting happiness and joy.

"Commandments . . . put us under a solemn obligation to develop gratitude and the spirit of thanksgiving. We should be thankful and express appreciation for all of our blessings."

(Marion G. Romney, "Gratitude and Thanksgiving," *Ensign*, November 1982).

Chapter 7
AN EXERCISE IN GRATITUDE

GRATITUDE CAN BE A HABIT. It literally becomes part of our natural behavior, even our character, and we will look to be grateful. This section has exercises we can do in order to practice being grateful, to make gratitude a habit in our lives.

Exercise #1: Stop what you're doing for a moment. Wherever you are, look around. Take note of all the things around you, and consider them from a grateful point of view. As I do this exercise today from my little study in the basement, I see many family pictures on the walls. I am grateful for my family and my sweetheart. I am grateful for my computer that Heavenly Father inspired someone to invent so I can do family history and so I can write my little books. I am grateful for the pictures in every direction, for the artists whose works surround my little desk with images of my beloved Savior and the sculptures that remind me of my Savior Jesus Christ. As I see my medicine sitting on the shelf, I am grateful for doctors. I'm grateful the Lord inspired the research scientists who created that medicine. I am grateful for my printer, even though it recently broke. I am grateful that I can order a new printer head to print my manuscript. I am especially grateful for one particular book sitting nearby, *The Teachings of the Prophet Joseph Smith*. Oh, how I love the Prophet Joseph. It was through him that the gospel was restored. I'm grateful for the goodness of God. I'm grateful for His tender mercies. I am grateful for the Sabbath day. I am grateful that I can partake of the sacrament. I am grateful that I can remember and renew all my covenants and pledge to keep the commandments. I am grateful for the Atonement of my Savior, which enables everything in my life.

These few minutes I took to take note of my blessings became a tender moment as my soul filled with gratitude and thanksgiving. I stopped, wrote a paragraph in my gratitude journal, and felt grateful yet again and good inside.

 Journaling Moment of Joy

Now take a moment to look around and record the things you are grateful for. Take a moment in FHE to try this exercise with your family.

With grateful eyes glistening, we see the miracle of life and the beauty of nature. Everything becomes a moment of gratitude that awakens our soul. We notice our breathing. We notice our heart beating. We notice our ears hearing the beauty of the sounds of nature. With these miracles at work, worry is dispelled, stress flees, and joy becomes the fruit of our lives. Gratitude is born of the heart, which is the center of the soul and the affection and feeling center of our very being. The feelings of our heart usually govern our actions, so the question is how do we teach ourselves and our children to be aware of and recognize the feelings of our hearts and act upon them?

I remember when we as a family went to a rest home to deliver some cake left over from our daughter Karie's wedding reception. We were all loaded with little pieces of cake, and I suggested that the older children could go by themselves. Steven, our oldest boy, asked me what to do. I explained, "Just go in and tell them we wanted to share some cake with them." He was a little timid, having never done this before, yet off he went. I could see the children down the long hall, going in and out of the rooms with smiles on their faces. I was a happy father because I could tell something was happening inside their hearts.

When we had all finished, Steven was nowhere to be found. We started looking for him, and as I walked down one of the side halls, I peeked into a room. There he was, the cake on the side table, with a very elderly lady holding his hand, saying, "Please don't leave me." Steven had been there a while, and although not sure what to do, he wouldn't leave her side. I called an attendant, and she came and helped the lady so Steven could come with us. Something happened that night inside my son's heart. He was changed forever. Ever since that day, he has always helped the special-needs children or those who are a little different. He has compassion for those who have misfortune in their lives. The experience changed his heart forever. Even today, thirty-eight years later, one of his special friends from high school will call him up, and Steven takes him to lunch. That night as we rode home from our family home evening activity, I asked how they felt about the experience. The response was overwhelmingly enthusiastic about how good they felt helping the elderly.

With children, helping them to process what they have learned from moments, gifts, or situations by asking them how they feel is key, as it precipitates the transfer to the grateful heart, and actions follow. Then gratitude becomes a logical, genuine, and natural expression, and they want to do it again because it feels so good.

As we look at creating a grateful heart, remember it takes time, and each person is different in their learning and growing process. We should all be virtuous and moral people, but the process of becoming is different for everyone. Required and demanded behavior doesn't help us change and show gratitude as well as understanding and appreciating the "why" and the "how."

The more we are grateful, the more we have to be grateful for. Like love, the more you give, the more you have. It never runs out, for it is self-replenishing. It is important as we focus on gratitude that we focus on the abundance we enjoy, on the blessings we receive. If our focus is on what we have rather than what we don't have, our lives will be better. Blessings of the present are to be remembered and recalled in times of trial and tribulation. Always remember there are many who do not have.

Practice Makes Perfect

Just as practicing any skill makes you more proficient, practicing gratitude is necessary to truly living with a grateful heart. Set aside a time, a place, and a way to express gratitude on a regular basis, in addition to expressing it during natural and inspired moments. When we practice and express gratitude, we will find that it softens our heart and exudes love to others. What we are radiates, and others will feel our love and recognize our gratitude. The goodness of God and the light of our Savior will come into their lives. We can thus become instruments in the Lord's hands to bring joy and happiness to others.

Oftentimes when we feel the Spirit during general conference or other wonderful meetings, we have a desire to do good. If we fail to act upon it in a matter of days, it is as if we really didn't receive it into our hearts. We must have enough gratitude for the lessons learned to act upon them or else it was just another meeting with no results. It is important that we don't just feel grateful but that we act upon those feelings with all diligence. If gratitude is deep enough, we will put into practice what we have learned. We will seek to please Heavenly Father and our Savior.

Practicing gratitude is much the same as practicing many other attributes or skills we learn. We exercise to become better runners or to have better health. We practice basketball to become better players. We practice hitting to be better batters. We practice the piano to be better musicians. Everything takes time and effort to improve. This is why consciously recalling our blessings daily in addition to recording them and expressing them to others brings the habit and joy of gratitude to our lives.

The Miracle of Expressing Gratitude Every Day

I was in the last stages of writing this book when I experienced a tender mercy of the Lord in my life. I had been praying for heavenly help in writing something that would inspire everyone to be grateful. The only reason I write is the hope that someone's life will be uplifted and edified and, above all, that it will be pleasing to my Heavenly Father. My son Steve introduced me to a new friend of his who really practices expressing gratitude. For years he has sent all kinds of cards and gifts on a regular basis, expressing gratitude for people who have affected his life in positive ways. He did this almost every day for many years, and now he does it every single day without fail. He expresses gratitude and thanksgiving, wishes people happy birthday, and gives them PIE (you remember—praise, inspiration, and encouragement). As I looked into his eyes, I could feel how much love he has for others. That is when he said the miraculous words, "Brother Ed, expressing gratitude has changed my life. This is what I do. This is who I am." His gratitude is overflowing because it is rooted in his heart. He shares his love every day as he seeks to uplift, nurture, help, and bless others. He is a perfect example of looking for the good and then expressing gratitude, bringing cheer, and sharing joy with all he associates with. He keeps a daily gratitude journal too. He is living proof of what I have attempted to write.

Chapter 8
THE SIN OF INGRATITUDE

THE LORD HAS COUNSELED, "AND in nothing doth man offend God, or against none is his wrath kindled, save those who confess not his hand in all things, and obey not his commandments" (D&C 59:21). If we fail to express gratitude and thanksgiving to God, we may be guilty of one of the greatest sins—the sin of ingratitude. President Ezra Taft Benson reminded us:

> The Prophet Joseph said at one time that one of the greatest sins of which the Latter-day Saints would be guilty is the sin of ingratitude. I presume most of us have not thought of that as a great sin. There is a great tendency for us in our prayers and in our pleadings with the Lord to ask for additional blessings. But sometimes I feel we need to devote

more of our prayers to expressions of gratitude and thanksgiving for blessings already received. We enjoy so much. (*God, Family, Country* [Salt Lake City: Deseret Book Company, 1974], 199)

President Joseph Fielding Smith wrote:

One of the greatest sins, both in magnitude and extent . . . is the sin of ingratitude. When we violate a commandment, no matter how small and insignificant we may think it to be, we show our ingratitude to our Redeemer. It is impossible for us to comprehend the extent of his suffering when he carried the burden of the sins of the whole world. . . . If we really understood and could feel even to a small degree, the love and gracious willingness on the part of Jesus Christ to suffer for our sins we would be willing to repent of all our transgressions and serve him. (*The Restoration of All Things* [Salt Lake City: Deseret Book Company, 1945], 199.)

If ingratitude can be considered one of the greatest sins, then gratitude should be considered one of the greatest virtues, even one of the cardinal virtues in life. Yet for all of its grave importance, far too often, gratitude is the forgotten virtue. This forgetfulness is expressed in the scriptures and in everyday life. Luke records a great example of this during the Lord's ministry on earth:

> As he [Christ] entered into a certain village, there met him ten men that were lepers, which stood afar off: And they lifted up their voices, and said, Jesus, Master, have mercy on us. And when he saw them, he said unto them, Go shew yourselves unto the priests. And it came to pass, that, as they went, they were cleansed. And one of them, when he saw that he was healed, turned back, and with a loud voice glorified God, And fell down on his face at his feet, giving him thanks: and he was a Samaritan. And Jesus answering said, Were there not ten cleansed? but where

> are the nine? There are not found that returned to give glory to God, save this stranger. And he said unto him, Arise, go thy way: thy faith hath made thee whole. (Luke 17:12–19)

The Lord immediately drew attention to the lack of gratitude for this miraculous healing. Leprosy was and is a hideous disease. It is contagious and disfiguring. In Christ's time, people with this condition became social outcasts, and being cured was rare. The leper was required to call out "unclean" to warn strangers of an approaching leper. The inflicted's life was horrible at best. To be healed immediately, in a moment, was not only a miracle but also a blessing beyond measure. The Savior cleansed and cured ten, yet *only one* expressed gratitude to the Lord! Did the others forget?

Paul taught, "Because that, when they knew God, they glorified him not as God, neither were thankful; but became vain in their imaginations, and their foolish heart was darkened" (Romans 1:21). Is it possible the cured lepers were so focused on themselves that they knew not their

God who had saved them? Similarly, we are often so excited about the blessing that we fail to stop in the moment to express gratitude to the giver. Time passes, and gratitude goes unexpressed.

Poet and minister Thomas Gibbons wrote in "When Jesus Dwelt" of the plight of ingratitude:

That man may last, but never lives,
Who much receives, but nothing gives;
Whom none can love, whom none can thank,—
Creation's blot, creation's blank.

I know of a man who gave several hundred gifts to coworkers in a common cause on two different occasions. There was a great relationship between them, and the giver of the gift simply wanted to show gratitude for their efforts. However, following the reception of the gift, very few expressed appreciation in any form at all. The giver was still happy but inwardly wondered if they had truly received, accepted, and applied the gift to their lives with a grateful heart. Both the giver and the receivers were denied the blessings of gratitude.

Journaling Moment of Joy

Even if years have passed, take a moment and record your feelings about past blessings, then convey that thought to the giver. Expressing gratitude, even years later, blesses lives.

The Greatest of All Gifts

The Lord teaches us of the dilemma of not accepting His gifts in gratitude: "For what doth it profit a man if a gift is bestowed upon him, and he receive not the gift? Behold, he rejoices not in that which is given unto him, neither rejoices in him who is the giver of the gift" (D&C 88:33). The greatest gift of all is the Atonement. If we do not accept in gratitude the Atonement of Christ, we will not enter into the covenants of the Lord's gospel.

> *The greatest gift of all is the Atonement.*

The importance of giving thanks has been taught from the beginning of time, when Adam was commanded to offer up burnt offerings in thanksgiving in similitude of our Savior's Atonement. The brother of Jared was chastised for failing to make an offering in thanksgiving: "And it came to pass at the end of four years that the Lord came again unto the brother of Jared, and stood in a cloud and talked with him. And for the space of three hours did the Lord talk with the brother of Jared, and chastened him because *he remembered not to call upon the name of the Lord*" (Ether 2:14, emphasis added). Here, calling on the name of the Lord referred not simply to praying to Him but to making a sacrificial offering of gratitude to the Him, which was in similitude of His sacrifice. It was also a form of worship. The sacrificial offering was a symbol for the atoning sacrifice of our Savior, and without the Atonement, all mankind would be lost forever. No wonder the Lord was upset with the brother of Jared for failing to lay hold of this saving power. Lack of gratitude is a serious sin. The good news is we can repent, just as the brother of Jared did:

> And the brother of Jared repented of the evil which he had done, and did call upon the name of the Lord for his brethren who were with him. And

> the Lord said unto him: I will forgive thee and thy brethren of their sins; but thou shalt not sin any more, for ye shall remember that my Spirit will not always strive with man; wherefore, if ye will sin until ye are fully ripe ye shall be cut off from the presence of the Lord. And these are my thoughts upon the land which I shall give you for your inheritance; for it shall be a land choice above all other lands. (Ether 2:15)

This offering was demonstrated throughout the Old Testament (see Genesis 4:4; Exodus 18:12; 29:18; 30:15; Leviticus 4:3; Numbers 6:14; 1 Samuel 13:9; Isaiah 56:7), and they were to be made in thanksgiving (see Leviticus 7:12; 22:29). King Benjamin and his people lived the law of Moses, "and they also took of the firstlings of their flocks, that they might offer sacrifice and burnt offerings according to the law of Moses; And also that they might give thanks to the Lord their God" (Mosiah 2:3–4). They continued this until the Resurrection of our Savior, when He taught the new law of sacrifice: "And ye shall offer up unto me no more the shedding of blood; yea, your sacrifices and your burnt offerings shall be done away, for I will accept none of your sacrifices and your burnt offerings. And ye shall offer for a sacrifice unto me a broken heart and a contrite spirit" (3 Nephi 9:19–20).

The Lord expects us to have grateful hearts and to offer prayers of thanksgiving. When we think about the laws of obedience, sacrifice, and consecration, we can readily see that thanksgiving is to be done with a pure heart and not performed grudgingly, else it would not be acceptable to God (see Moroni 7:8). The words Shakespeare places in the utterance of King Henry still resonate in our hearts: "Let never day nor night unhallowed pass, But still remember what the Lord hath done" (*Henry VI, Part 2*, 2.1.83–84).

Journaling Moment of Joy

Ponder on Shakespeare's words, and then record your feelings. Remembering to be grateful will sow the seeds of a grateful heart.

We can overcome the sin of ingratitude as we ponder the blessings of the Atonement in our lives. This, you recall, is why Moroni encouraged and exhorted us to ponder the mercy of the Lord in our lives (see Moroni 10:3). This is what Jacob was attempting to do when he taught of the Atonement in 2 Nephi 9. This is why my students read this chapter for thirty days straight so their hearts could feel the depth of the power of the Atonement in their lives. This is what Amulek was teaching when he said:

> For it is expedient that an atonement should be made; for according to the great plan of the Eternal God there must be an atonement made, or else all mankind must unavoidably perish; yea, all are hardened; yea, all are fallen and are lost, and must perish except it be through the atonement which it is expedient should be made. For it is expedient that there should be a great and last sacrifice; yea, not a sacrifice of man, neither of beast, neither of any manner of fowl; for

it shall not be a human sacrifice; but it must be an infinite and eternal sacrifice. (Alma 34:9–10)

Until we are grateful for the Atonement of the Lord, the seed of gratitude will not take root and flourish into a tree of gratitude. The Atonement is the enabling power of a grateful heart.

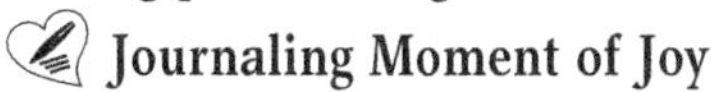

Record your feelings about your Savior and His infinite Atonement.

Chapter 9

ROADBLOCKS TO A GRATEFUL HEART

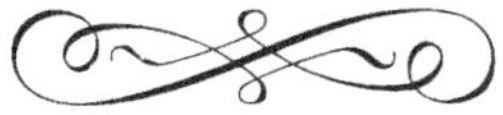

THERE ARE MANY ROADBLOCKS TO having feelings of gratitude. Anything that makes us think of ourselves will tend to block expressions of gratitude. Feelings of jealousy, anger, envy, bitterness, dislike, and hatred will block gratitude, but there is an antidote, and that is forgiveness coupled with charity and compassion. When we are truly grateful, forgiveness becomes a byproduct of our heart. We have compassion and even pity for others because of their misdeeds. Forgiveness frees us from the baggage of anger because it is not only the Christlike thing to do, but it also brings freedom from negative emotions to our soul. It is an act of gratitude, for the Lord has forgiven us, and thus we are motivated to forgive others. We find that forgiveness leads us to peace and helps us gain victory over ours and others' sins.

I remember the first time as a priesthood leader that I faced the challenge of helping a sister in my ward overcome another's sin of abuse. Her roommates mentioned how she would remain in the apartment and cry. Other friends sought to assist but didn't know what to do. The matter finally came to my attention, and I sought a time to interview her. As I sat with her to begin the visit, she started to cry. I tried to console her but to no avail. I thought she might need a little time to be alone, so I stood to excuse myself. As I did so, I raised my hand to the side of my head, and she cowered in her chair. Devastated, I discerned immediately the situation and expressed my sympathy and love. She seemed calmed, and we began to talk. As we visited, it came out that her father had physically and sexually abused her. I wept. We wept together. We talked of life and her future. We talked of her desire to once again be happy. I asked her, "Do you want to be happy?" Of course her response was positive. Then I asked if she would do what I asked her to do so she could be happy. She willingly said yes.

The Lord and the Holy Spirit direct and guide encounters like this, and I was truly led by the Spirit, not knowing beforehand the things I should say or do (see 1 Nephi 4:6). Oh, the goodness of God. I said, "Call your father and frankly forgive him. Encourage him to see the bishop immediately so he can begin the process of repentance." She agreed to do it. We prayed and planned our next visit.

Over time, the roommates mentioned that good things were happening. The distressed sister became more positive and upbeat. The enabling power of the Atonement was taking effect. She was being healed. She became enthusiastic, friendly, and outgoing. It was a miracle. She later returned home, married a wonderful young man in the temple, and now has several children. Her life is good. Yes, there is a way, and it is in and through our Savior Jesus Christ. He is always there. We must call upon God so the nurturing and succoring power of our Savior's sacrifice become efficacious in our lives.

To those who have been sinned against, *forgiveness* is the watchword to live by. Repentance through Christ the Lord is the only way for those who have sinned. We must look to the Lord for strength, knowing and believing that the Lord Himself has suffered through opposition and temptation of the highest order and magnitude. Sometimes we struggle with expressing love and gratitude. All too often we get set in our ways, and we focus on the negative things of life. What's wrong with this? Everything! Those who do not have eyes to see usually see the negative. We need to do what Alma suggested: "Look to God and live" (Alma 37:47). If we look to the goodness and mercy of God, we can live not only in gratitude but also in the image of Christ. To have gratitude, we need new eyes to see, new ears to hear, and new hearts to feel. Our souls must embrace the goodness and mercies of God and our Savior Jesus Christ.

Sorrow and adversity, though difficult to face and overcome, often create the moment when gratitude is born. We see out of different eyes. Life's true purpose and values come flooding to the surface. Our perception is broadened, and things that matter most are front and center in

Sorrow and adversity, though difficult to face and overcome, often create the moment when gratitude is born.

our lives. It is at this juncture that we often see blessings gone unnoticed, and then gratitude fills our hearts. In the sorrow of death comes gratitude for life. In the sorrow of being apart comes gratitude for the memories of togetherness. In adversity, we come to see blessings never appreciated before because we had never been without. It often seems that we don't appreciate a blessing until it is taken away through adversity. In sorrow and adversity, gratitude can be the fruit of our hearts and minds if they are soft and easily entreated.

Gratitude has a difficult time when competition raises its ugly head, when comparison raises its ever-increasing probe into our hearts. Gratitude flourishes when we see what we have and are grateful for it. It's been noted that those who have, want more still continually. They never stop. More creates an insatiable desire for more. Gratitude is not destructive but creative—enough becomes enough, and we are made free from the devastating desire of greed.

My sweetheart, in her Church assignment as general Primary president, had the privilege of visiting many countries where poverty prevailed and it was a struggle just to survive. Upon her return home from one such trip, we called the children around, and she told the story of a very happy family whose home was a shack with a dirt floor and no running water. How can people in a country of little material wealth be so happy? How can a mother with a few children, a hard-working husband, a small hut with a thatched roof and dirt floor in the middle of the jungle, little clothing, and barely enough food say to my sweetheart when she was making a visit, "We are so happy"? It was the miracle of gratitude, gratitude for what she had. It was gratitude for the gospel in their lives. This kind of gratitude will bring joy no matter your circumstances, and life will be sweet.

When people don't express gratitude, there are reasons. If we are aware of these concerns, we will be more compassionate and better able to help others and ourselves express gratitude.

Journaling Moment of Joy

> *Consider all the things that bring us gratitude. If we are grateful, we don't need things to bring us happiness.*

Record your feelings about the above statement. Do you really believe it? How do "things" affect your life?

Reasons for Not Expressing Gratitude

There are many things that hold us or others back from feeling grateful and expressing our gratitude. As we interact with others, there are times when we feel underappreciated or taken for granted. We can be more compassionate and forgiving if we realize we may not understand another's reasons for their apparent lack of gratitude. As you read the following list, be willing to honestly hold a mirror up to yourself and reflect on possible roadblocks to your own ability to live with a grateful heart.

Roadblock 1: Failure to count one's blessings

When we fail to look for our blessings, we shut off the fuel source for a grateful heart. Our eyes are not attuned to seeing our blessings, and our hearts and minds will not have an attitude of gratitude. Without an attitude of gratitude, we will fail to express gratitude.

Roadblock 2: Not pondering on the goodness and mercy of the Lord and His infinite Atonement

If we fail to ponder on the goodness and mercy of God, our minds and hearts will not be consumed with gratitude for what the Lord has done for us. This is why we must ponder on the Lord's infinite Atonement (see Moroni 10:3). This gratitude and thanksgiving to God is the beginning of having a grateful heart. It is like having a living well of thanksgiving springing forth from within our souls so that we have an overwhelming desire to express gratitude not only to Heavenly Father and our Savior but also to all mankind.

Roadblock 3: A skewed perception of life

If our values are not in harmony with goodness, if our past experience has been distressing, or if our attitude is negative, our perception will be skewed. We will not only fail to see the things we should be grateful for, but we will also fail to feel those things that will bring gratitude into our hearts. Expressing gratitude will be the furthest thing from our minds.

Roadblock 4: Unawareness of the gift

If we are not aware of a gift or have failed to receive the gift, then we will not feel gratitude; therefore, even the thought of gratitude will not reside in our minds and hearts.

Roadblock 5: Neglect to look for the good in life or others

Looking for the good opens the door to feelings of gratitude. Seeing the good touches our hearts with the swelling motions of thanksgiving, and thus we seek to express gratitude. As I looked at my sweetheart's garden and all of its beauty, I immediately expressed my gratitude to her for all she had done to make life so good and her garden so magnificent.

Roadblock 6: Pride and selfishness

Pride and selfishness are the killers of all the attributes and virtues of goodness. It is "me" centered. It is selfish. It looks for self-aggrandizement rather than gratitude for others. Humility will always conquer pride and help us look toward others with thanksgiving and love.

Roadblock 7: Low self-esteem and low self-confidence

If, for whatever reason, we lack self-esteem, self-worth, and self-confidence, the results are devastating. We do not function well socially or have the ability to communicate and express our feelings. We feel inadequate. Until we know who we are and what we were destined to be as children of God, we will be unable to express gratitude.

Roadblock 8: Feelings of inadequacy in communicating

Communication is the bedrock of relationships. It is a skill and an art. It takes effort to learn. If our heart is right, we can learn to be grateful. Like all skills, if we simply try to express gratitude, we will learn it over time. Patience is the virtue of power—don't give up on yourself!

Roadblock 9: Feeling overwhelmed or stressed

If we feel overwhelmed, hope will have a difficult time residing in our hearts and minds. Frustration causes us to not function at a high level because we are concentrating so much on just getting through the day that there doesn't seem to be time to look for the good, let alone express gratitude. Organizing every needful thing and reassessing what matters most can help with being overwhelmed. Patience and time are our allies.

Roadblock 10: Hardness of heart

Hardness of heart can be from trauma to our souls, a skewed perception of life, pride having built a nest inside our hearts, a negative attitude . . . and the list can go on. We choose how we react to all of these apparent causes of being hardhearted. We can choose to have an easily entreated heart. We can choose to turn to God in our trials and traumas of life. We can change our perception, let our hearts be humble, and have an attitude of gratitude.

Roadblock 11: Fear of being indebted

Sometimes people are afraid of the consequences of expressing gratitude, fearing that the receiver will feel indebted to them in a relationship. Sometimes people do kind deeds for us, and we are afraid to express gratitude because by so doing we acknowledge indebtedness to the giver. Some people simply avoid perceived ties of any sort and withhold giving or receiving expressions of gratitude. Indebtedness to God brings forth an increase of gratitude.

Roadblock 12: Perfectionism

If we expect too much from others, we will never be able to feel grateful toward anyone because they do not meet our expectations. Gratitude for effort and doing one's best is more important than a perfect performance. Life is full of imperfect people. Look for the good.

Roadblock 13: Never having had the joy of receiving, giving, and/or expressing thanks

A person who has never tasted gratitude and thanksgiving often has difficulty expressing gratitude. Those who have never felt love have difficulty expressing love. This is why it is so important to teach children to express and feel gratitude at an early age.

Roadblock 14: Not recognizing the need to appreciate others

Sometimes we become cynical and callous concerning the feelings of others. This will take the life out of living. Whether we recognize it or not, the greatest need in all the world is to be loved or to receive gratitude. The greatest joy is expressing love or expressing gratitude.

Roadblock 15: Fear of man (worrying about what others think)

Fear of what others may think often makes the real us fail to live up to our potential. We become afraid that others will think our expression of gratitude is phony or manipulative. Until we are willing to stand up for what we are, we will always be swayed and pressured by our peers—and this is a huge mistake. The fear of man can be debilitating. We are in charge of our lives. Do what is right. The power of gratitude lifts every soul it touches.

Roadblock 16: Lack of respect or reverence for others and for things

This is a major barrier in expressing gratitude. Respect and reverence for others and things are precursors to developing a grateful heart and the courage to express gratitude. Young children who are taught respect and reverence seem to be endowed with an attitude of gratitude, and expressing thanks is a natural response.

Roadblock 17: Reluctance to invest the time and effort (impatience)

Expressing gratitude takes effort. If we feel overloaded and restricted in our time commitments, expressing gratitude becomes something else on a long list of to-dos. If only we could see that to say "Thank you," "You are so kind," or "You have made my day" can make the difference in someone's life. It takes fewer than sixty seconds to write a note or an e-mail expressing thanks. Making the time is the making of a new life filled with gratitude and love.

Roadblock 18: Lack of empathy

Empathy is part of compassion and love. It is caring and responding to another's feelings and situation. If we don't care, then expressing gratitude would be dishonest. It would border on hypocrisy. We should seek to put ourselves in another's situation, learn to listen in hopes to understand. The greater our empathy, the greater our capacity to express gratitude.

There can be many roadblocks to feeling and expressing gratitude. The important thing is to do something about it so we don't end up never knowing happiness because we have never felt gratitude.

Journaling Moment of Joy

Roadblocks become gates to the future when we address them and seek to do better. Daunting but doable—and worth every effort. Write your plan to overcome roadblocks in your gratitude journal and look at it daily.

Chapter 10
BLESSINGS OF A GRATEFUL HEART

Gratitude Blesses Our Lives

WHEN WE EXPRESS GRATITUDE TO another person, a feeling of unity and togetherness is created. A bond is established through expressions of love and acceptance of that service. Both hearts are touched, and with continued nurturing, the relationship is deepened.

Having a grateful heart evokes the power to turn . . .

Adversity into opportunity—Gratitude for the opportunity to grow.

Discouragement into hope—Gratitude for the power and strength of Christ in our lives.

Envy into charity—Gratitude for the feeling that enough is enough so envy will flee.

Enmity into unity—Gratitude for the love of God that destroys contention.

Sorrow into joy—Gratitude for an eternal perspective that changes sorrow into life eternal.

Roadblock into a labor of love—Gratitude for all things that make work a small price for success.

Jealousy into love and admiration—Gratitude for love so jealousy will disappear.

Self-condemnation into self-worth and self-confidence—Gratitude for our divine nature.

Random acts of kindness into continuing and constant acts of charity—Gratitude for the ability to become what we can.

Endowment of light into a power to do good—Gratitude for receiving power through the Holy Ghost to do good.

Spiritual weakness into strength—Gratitude for invoking humility and faith so we can be strengthened in the Lord.

Restlessness into peace—Gratitude for the Lord for bringing peace only He can give.

Doubt into faith—Gratitude for the goodness of the Lord, which helps us increase our faith in Him.

Helplessness into pleading prayers—Gratitude for the ability to fall to our knees and petition God.

Trials into blessings—Gratitude for seeing beyond the trial to the promised blessings.

Hatred into love—Gratitude for building charity, in which hatred cannot exist.

Pride into humility and reverence—Gratitude for its being the precursor to humility and reverence, so thus pride is destroyed.

Greed into generosity—Gratitude for its ability to overwhelm greed because enough is enough, and generosity is its byproduct.

Selfishness into caring for others—Gratitude for its birth to selflessness and thinking about and caring for others first.

Never forget, in every trial, in every moment of opposition, and in every trying temptation and difficult moment in life that there will be a ray of light that will teach us the blessing of the moment, such that gratitude will fill our souls with thanksgiving. We must learn to take the time to address each one so gratitude and other virtues can empower us.

Journaling Moment of Joy

Record your feelings about the empowerment you discover when gratitude consumes your heart and soul, changing your heart forever.

Church Leaders Understand the Nature and Power of a Grateful Heart

We are constantly counseled about the importance of gratitude. President Howard W. Hunter has counseled us, "Happiness is not complete unless accompanied by gratitude. . . . Happiness and joy from blessings are never complete until there is a deep feeling of gratitude within oneself which moves an expression of appreciation" (*The Teachings of Howard W. Hunter*, edited by Clyde J. Williams [Salt Lake City: Bookcraft, 1997], 93).

> *Happiness is not complete unless accompanied by gratitude.*

President Hugh B. Brown wrote:

How rich and radiant is the soul of a man who has a thankful heart. His gratitude increases with his unfolding awareness of himself, the universe, and his Creator. Appreciation, like love, enriches both giver and receiver, and, when spontaneously expressed in word or deed, reveals a depth and delicacy of fine-grain character. True gratitude is motivated by a recognition of favors received. Its counterfeit is fawning anticipation of favors to come. . . . He who has a thankful heart and cultivates the spirit of appreciation, will find much to be grateful for each hour of every day. . . . We should make a necklace of the pearls of our many blessings and wear it constantly. Its beads, when gratefully counted, will gain luster and be magnified when seen through thankful eyes. This counting of blessings will discover and emphasize good fortune, ease life's yoke, lighten its burden. The spirit of thanksgiving will spread its contagion to all within reach of its radiation. . . . They who show their gratitude to God by serving their fellow men will be entitled to hear his word: "Ye have done it unto me.". . . Sincere and heartfelt appreciation is a spiritual attribute often found among those who seemingly or by comparison have little to be grateful for. But they who possess this virtue are rich indeed as in meekness and modesty they express their gratitude by word and life and willing service, without any thought of possible returns; they thereby enrich the lives of others. A truly thankful person need not be a profound thinker, an outstanding artist, an eminent scientist or be rich in worldly possessions, but his spirit of appreciation will enable him to live abundantly. (*Continuing the Quest* [Salt Lake City: Deseret Book Company, 1961], 449–451.)

The Temple Is a Place of Thanksgiving

When the Saints were commanded to prepare a House of the Lord, the Lord used compelling language that characterized this edifice as a place of thanksgiving and instruction. Note the precise wording and the promised outcome:

> Verily I say unto you, that it is my will that a house should be built unto me in the land of Zion, like unto the pattern which I have given you.
>
> Yea, let it be built speedily, by the tithing of my people.
>
> Behold, this is the tithing and the sacrifice which I, the Lord, require at their hands, that there may be a house built unto me for the salvation of Zion—
>
> For a place of thanksgiving for all saints, and for a place of instruction for all those who are called to the work of the ministry in all their several callings and offices;
>
> That they may be perfected in the understanding of their ministry, in

> theory, in principle, and in doctrine, in all things pertaining to the kingdom of God on the earth, the keys of which kingdom have been conferred upon you.
>
> And inasmuch as my people build a house unto me in the name of the Lord, and do not suffer any unclean thing to come into it, that it be not defiled, my glory shall rest upon it. (D&C 97:10–15)

A grateful heart is the beginning of an attitude that empowers us to try and to become. We must not forget that our gratitude and love will increase through the enabling power of the infinite Atonement (see Alma 7:11–12), which empowers us to do all things through faith in Christ (see Moroni 10:23).

As we come to the end of this book, it is important to make note of some profound truths. Every one of Heavenly Father's children has within them the light of Christ. They know good from evil. These same people (myself included) all want to feel good. Everyone wants to be happy. Every survey taken about the desires and wishes of the hearts of men all over the world comes up with the same universal answer: I would like to be happy. Happiness is our quest. The Prophet Joseph reminded us that the design of our existence is to be happy. Some seek a false state of happiness with self-aggrandizement through gluttony, sex, alcohol, and a variety of other addictions that fail. Others seek to exercise constantly for the euphoric feelings they enjoy. Everyone seeks to find a principle or two that will bring a sense of euphoria and well-being, even a feeling of happiness to their present situation. I have spent much time reading every account of gratitude I could find. I have read several books on this subject, and I have discovered many authors who acknowledge extremely varied beliefs—everything from atheism to agnosticism to born-again Christianity. The important fact about the light of Christ is *all people who embrace a true principle and live it experience the fruits from it regardless of their religious affiliation.* The truth is that gratitude is an eternal principle. It is centered in our Heavenly Father and our Savior. It can become rooted in our souls forever. Those who live it and apply it throughout their lives harvest the empowerment of gratitude. They are blessed to the extent that they practice the principle of gratitude. We learn from the Lord, "There is a law, irrevocably decreed in heaven before the foundations of this world, upon which all blessings are predicated—And when we obtain any blessing from God, it is by obedience to that law upon which it is predicated" (D&C 130:20–21). We give credit to God for all things and are continually drawn to Him through His expressions of love and mercy toward us.

The virtue of gratitude precedes blessings of a joyful and a happy life. The Lord, personally and through His prophets, has done all in His power to help us remember the goodness and mercy of God so we can discover the empowering nature of gratitude.

This process of becoming and showing gratitude begins with our thoughts. Remember, "As [a man] thinketh in his heart, so is he" (Proverbs 23:7). Let us ponder gratitude and thanksgiving, ponder and meditate on the goodness of God and our many blessings in all aspects of our lives. As we dwell on these gifts, our gratitude will begin to swell within our hearts. And as we express our gratitude through our actions, slowly but surely, our hearts will change and become a grateful well springing up with life-giving power, resulting in an enriched and happy life filled with joy and thanksgiving.

Journaling Moment of Joy

When we live in thanksgiving daily, our journals will become a source of strength as we take time to record and reread those precious words that bind us to our Heavenly Father, our Savior, and those we love. Commit to continue recognizing and recording your many blessings throughout your life, and you will reap the blessings of the heavenly virtue of gratitude.

About the Author

J. Pinegar is the author of more than sixty nfiction books, audio-books, and talks.

He has had the opportunity to teach at Brigham ung University, the Orem Institute of Religion, the ovo MTC, various seminaries, and BYU Education eek. He has been blessed with the opportunity to serve in ny positions of leadership within The Church of us Christ of Latter-day Saints, most recently serving as Manti Temple president.

He and his wife, Pat, are the parents of eight, grand- ents of thirty-eight, and great-grandparents of twenty- e. Ed and his wife live in Orem, Utah.